AUG 0 4 2004

W9-ACU-684

AMERICA THE BROKE

How the Reckless Spending of

the White House and Congress

Is Bankrupting Our Country

and Destroying Our Children's Future

AMERICA THE BROKE

GERALD J. SWANSON, Ph.D.

NEW YORK   LONDON   TORONTO   SYDNEY   AUCKLAND

A CURRENCY BOOK
PUBLISHED BY DOUBLEDAY
a division of Random House, Inc.

CURRENCY is a trademark of Random House, Inc., and
DOUBLEDAY is a registered trademark of Random House, Inc.

Book design by Tina Thompson

Cataloging-in-Publication Data is on file with the Library of Congress
ISBN: 0-385-51304-6

PRINTED IN THE UNITED STATES OF AMERICA

First Edition: August 2004

SPECIAL SALES
Currency Books are available at special discounts for bulk purchases for
sales promotions or premiums. Special editions, including personalized
covers, excerpts of existing books, and corporate imprints, can be created
in large quantities for special needs. For more information, write to
Special Markets, Currency Books, specialmarkets@randomhouse.com.
10 9 8 7 6 5 4 3 2 1

To Gwen with love—Thank you for always being there!
And the other loves of my life:
Scott & Rhonda
Laura & Bart
Grant, Grace, Jack, Nick & Kate

CONTENTS

ACKNOWLEDGMENTS

Many thanks to the incredible Helen Rees, my literary agent. Her commitment to this project—and this topic—made this book possible.

Also invaluable to this project: the writers, editors, designers, and researchers at Wordworks—Donna Carpenter, Maurice Coyle, Ruth Hlavacek, Larry Martz, Cindy Sammons, Robert Shnayerson, Matthew Polluck, and Robert Stock.

Finally, thanks to the indomitable and skilled Roger Scholl, our editor at Doubleday.

WHAT COULD DESTROY America?

One four-letter word: debt.

I didn't intend to write another book on the deficit and debt. I'd already written one.

In 1992, with the national deficit at its highest in U.S. history and our debt rising to a staggering trillion dollars, Harry Figgie and I wrote *Bankruptcy 1995*, warning of the imminent collapse of our country within three years' time if our leaders did not take the immediate steps to correct it. The book became a *New York Times* best-seller for more than nine months, selling more than 300,000 copies. But a miraculous thing happened. President Clinton and Congress, both Democrats and Republicans alike, heeded (some of) our advice and exercised a certain degree of fiscal restraint. Taxes were raised; spending, while not cut back, at least remained constant; and the economy began to boom. Throughout Clinton's years in office, the deficit was reduced each year, until, in his last two years, the government achieved surpluses. He even began paying down a portion of the debt. Problem solved.

But to my astonishment and consternation, in three short years our new President, George W. Bush, and his determined tax cutters, working with a Republican-controlled Congress, have unraveled eight years of fiscal responsibility. Through increased spending on domestic programs, defense, and entitlements, and two historic tax cuts, we are now, in 2004, projected to have the largest single deficit in history. The Bush Administration projects a $521 billion gap between the revenues our government takes in and what it spends. And, as I'll point out later in the book, even this inflated figure is grossly understated. To be sure, President Bush has had to cope with several major crises—the recession of 2001, the terrible tragedy of 9/11, the wars in Afghanistan and Iraq, as well as an ongoing war against terrorism.

Wars are expensive. But never before has an American president attempted to enact a major tax cut (much less two of them) while fighting a costly war. Every wartime President before him has, out of fiscal necessity, *raised* taxes. And George W. Bush has led us through *two* wars (and an ongoing occupation in Iraq). One can debate the geopolitical necessity of invading Iraq. I don't claim to have any special insights to offer. But on a fiscal level, the cost of the Iraq war in 2003 was a powerful shock to our economy. And the Administration makes no attempt to pay for that cost with offsetting cuts elsewhere—or even to include all the massive costs of the war in the budget. To me, that is irresponsible.

Our current national debt stands at $7.3 trillion. And it is rising by the minute. Divided per capita, it comes to $24,910 *per person*. Sooner or later, we have to stop the growth and start paying down our debt. Until that day comes, the interest will continue to eat up more and more of our tax dollars.

Add in consumer debt, which is more than doubling every 10 years, and our debt rises to $31,748 for every man, woman, and child. Tack on our mortgage debt of $7 trillion, and the number jumps to an astonishing $55,634.

Shocking, yes. But even more shocking is that our government lies about the commitments it makes in our names.

The Bush Administration, in collusion with Congress, has obfuscated the actual cost of rebuilding Iraq (perhaps by hundreds of billions of dollars). It hid more than $100 billion of its own estimate of the future cost of the Medicare drug benefits Congress passed in 2003. It "borrows" more than $150 billion a year from the Social Security "trust fund," magically turns that theft into federal budget revenues, and merrily spends your retirement savings. By the broadest calculation yet, our nation's total future obligation, in current dollars, is at least $44.2 trillion. It is a figure comprehensible only to mathematicians and astronomers, so let me translate: It means each and every American owes $150,829 in long-term tax obligations.

Add our per-capita national debt to our individual consumer debt and mortgage debt, and, as the chart below illustrates, every single American owes $181,553. For a family of four, that's a collective obligation of $726,212.

Of course, few American families own $726,212 in any form. How, then, will the government raise the trillions it's committed to

What We Really Owe

Billions			
$190,000			
$180,000			$181,553 —
$170,000			
$160,000			
$150,000			
$140,000			
$130,000			
$120,000			
$110,000			
$90,000			
$80,000			
$70,000			
$60,000			
$50,000			
$40,000			
$30,000	$24,910	$31,748	
$20,000			
$10,000			
$9,000			
	National Debt per Capita	Plus Consumer Debt	Plus Future Gov't. Commitments

spend, as well as the trillions more it isn't admitting it will spend? It will borrow. And borrow. And borrow. In so doing, it will pay more and more interest, consuming more and more of our tax dollars.

And one day soon, our government will suddenly run out of cash, unable to meet its payments, leaving the United States as bankrupt as any banana republic. We are far more vulnerable than most Americans realize. Only 23 years ago, in 1981, when interest rates last took off and rose to 20 percent, the total national debt was relatively modest—just over $1 trillion. Now, with a debt of $7.3 trillion, if interest rates were to hit just 18 percent, it would take every nickel collected in income taxes just to pay the interest on our existing debt. There would be no money left for defense, or homeland security, or education, or Social Security.

This scenario is hardly fiction. That the United States of America can literally go broke is no longer a fantasy but a likelihood—unless we stop the train now speeding us to Armageddon. If we do not get our financial house in order, and soon, I am convinced our great nation will collapse in a very short time under the weight of its financial obligations. I believe we can prevent the catastrophe: That's what this book is about—a cry from the heart for millions to join in forcing that calamitous train to a screeching halt.

History teaches that, sooner or later, all great nations perish. According to eighteenth-century Scottish historian Alexander Tytler, the average life span of leading civilizations is just 200 years. If true, the United States, at 200-plus years, may be living on borrowed time. Yes, we are still the world's undisputed superpower. But we are frittering away the economic strength that supports our dominance. In a very short time, we could go from being a superpower to becoming super-powerless.

Tytler foresaw the explanation for our present plight. "A democracy is always temporary in nature," he wrote. "It simply cannot exist as a permanent form of government," because, sooner or later, "voters discover that they can vote themselves generous gifts from the Public Treasury. From that moment on," Tytler observed, "the majority always votes for the candidates who promise the most benefits from the Public Treasury, with the result that every democracy will always collapse due to loose fiscal policy."

That's precisely what we Americans have been doing to ourselves. With few exceptions, our political leaders, Republicans and Democrats alike, have abandoned all pretense of fiscal responsibility. Spending is out of control, further ballooning the highest national debt in the history of the world. As I will show later, our current plight could touch off a world financial crisis and another Great Depression.

Before researching *Bankruptcy 1995,* I had never taken more than a conscientious citizen's interest in national politics. But my experience in writing the book opened my eyes to what really goes on in Washington. I realized how deeply addicted our leaders are to spending your money and mine—and our children's—without even pretending to care about the consequences for our grandchildren. I am writing again in the hope and belief that when the people of this country truly grasp the deadly threat that lies before us, they will act to reclaim the legacy of self-reliance and responsibility that has made America great.

The federal government has become our nation's foremost growth industry; the cost of running it, which came to $33 per person back in 1930, has multiplied by a factor of 172, to $5,700 a year today for every person in the United States. Worse yet, we are putting more and more of that bill on our national tab. Our expenses have overwhelmed revenues. The resulting tower of debt is wobbling dangerously over our heads. If this crisis isn't addressed soon, it will ruin our country.

Alexander Tytler, whose ideas are sadly neglected these days, made another observation worth pondering. Since the Athenian Republic two millennia ago, he wrote, all democracies have progressed through the same stages: "From bondage to spiritual faith; from spiritual faith to great courage; from courage to liberty; from liberty to abundance; from abundance to selfishness; from selfishness to complacency; from complacency to apathy; from apathy to dependence; from dependence back again into bondage."

From today's perspective, the United States is somewhere in the latter stages of this great cycle. Our Pilgrim ancestors found the faith to deliver themselves from persecution in England, and then the courage to tame a wilderness. Their descendants inherited their courage and independence, and waged the desperate fight to claim their liberty and lay the groundwork for an abundance that would astonish the world. But abundance can produce selfishness, self-indulgence, greed, complacency, and apathy, until liberty itself is in danger.

In the 1970s, selfishness began to tarnish the postwar abundance of the 1950s and 1960s, followed by the aptly named "me generation" decade of the 1980s. Then came the long boom of the 1990s, which gave rise to the dot-com stock bubble and the greed and corporate fraud that destroyed Enron, Tyco, WorldCom, and other high-flying companies.

Today, complacency threatens our national well-being yet again. While politicians squabble endlessly over tax cuts and entitlement programs, pork-barrel spending and special favors for campaign contributors, our citizens seem indifferent to the growing wreckage. There are no appeals from our elected leaders to Americans to sacrifice for the common good. Washington's fiscal recklessness has resulted in deficits as far as the eye can see. Will we have to plunge into national bankruptcy before our leaders act?

Already our leaders depend on domestic and foreign creditors to keep our government afloat. Sooner or later, our creditors will demand repayment. When we can't comply, Tytler's cycle will be complete: We will be back in bondage. The second chapter of this book paints a frightening picture of how such a collapse might look and feel to a middle-class American family.

Is it already too late? Is a crash inevitable? No. Our great nation can still avert calamity. We have always been a resourceful, resilient, and lucky country, and we will need all of that to survive the looming economic crisis. But we citizens first have to see the truth and find the determination and self-reliance to act on it. We need to tell our government leaders in no uncertain terms that their days at the public trough are over. We need to regain control over the budget—quickly. Together, we can do it. But time is short. This election year offers perhaps the last chance to persuade our leaders to change their course and act responsibly. In the final reckoning, it's up to us to do what's needed to save America's future.

PART ONE

IMPENDING DISASTER

CHAPTER 1

MARCHING TOWARD FISCAL ARMAGEDDON

IS AMERICA STILL economically healthy and wealthy?

Can we still trust our leaders with our lives, our liberties, our pocketbooks, our children's future?

How I wish we could say yes to the above.

But the sober truth is more chilling: The people we elected to run our country are bankrupting it instead.

They are literally spending more than we have at a runaway rate, like a locomotive steaming out of control. If we don't stop them, they will achieve what Adolf Hitler, Nikita Khrushchev, and Osama bin Laden never could: the destruction of American prosperity and the American Dream.

Harsh words, but I mean every one.

I'm talking about a chain of fiscal stupidities that could soon change your world forever. I'm talking about your job vanishing to Bangalore, your bank account emptied, your stocks in free fall.

I'm talking about your house on the market for a third of its former value with no buyers, your pension reduced to nothing, your monthly Social Security check too small to cover your rent or mortgage payment—assuming the government can still send you a check.

I'm talking about this blessed nation plunging blindly into insolvency. And why? Because our leaders—the people you and I elected to safeguard America's bounty—have squandered our country's money on schemes that would rightly land any nonpolitician behind bars.

Yes, our leaders: all those high-minded presidents, distinguished congresspersons, dedicated White House staffers—vast choirs of political opportunists singing hymns to rectitude while slicing and dicing pork from ever more specious national budgets.

Under cover of grandiose visions and national emergencies (most recently, our wars in Afghanistan and Iraq, in tandem with an economic slump), they have run up the government's yearly deficit—already more than $500 billion and rising in the year 2004 alone—in a binge of federal spending that is wildly out of control. Accordingly, the cost of borrowing more and more money to cover spending we can't pay for has itself veered out of control. Even at present low interest rates, the burden of paying ever more interest to finance ever-bigger yearly deficits can only accelerate the growth in the overall national debt itself. The result virtually guarantees national insecurity. If interest rates go up, as they must, we face actual insolvency. Yet our leaders blandly predict steady loan repayments ahead—without setting aside a penny to back up their assurances. Who are they fooling? Us—293 million plucked pigeons.

But what about those budget surpluses we were running in 1998 and 1999? Weren't they supposed to add up to more than $5 trillion in the next decade? Yes. But since then they've vanished like the morning mist, and the bright light of day reveals deficits stretching as far as the eye can see. While pledging fiscal discipline ("If Congress will not show spending restraint, I will enforce spending restraint"), President George W. Bush has cast aside a bipartisan commitment to balanced budgets and debt reduction adopted during the Clinton Administration. It's as if the Republicans, once exemplars of fiscal conservatism, have undergone some sort of gender change. President Bush has unapologetically run up a tab of new, unpaid-for initiatives, tax cuts, and debt service that, all told, will increase the deficit by an estimated $6.5 trillion over the next decade.

In plain English, our country is headed for national bankruptcy.

THE PATH TO POVERTY

Years and years of what amounts to pawning the family jewels to buy luxury cars and yachts have left the federal government in the kind of hock that used to send debtors to prison. As in most falls from grace, every wrong move has created worse ones, hastening and magnifying the dangers we face. Even so, the government's fundamental wrong move is clear—runaway spending. In the coming pages, I describe the financial Armageddon our country is striding toward at breakneck speed, along with charts showing the minefields ahead.

- **WE'RE SPENDING TOO MUCH.**

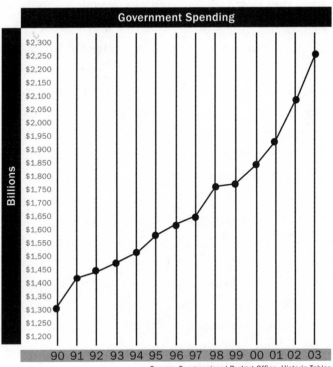

Source: Congressional Budget Office. Historic Tables

Washington insiders spout a lingo too exotic for mere voters, but the one word they never use—frugal—is too exotic for politicians. It means the great old virtue of economizing, of living within one's means. Hence the phenomenon of the mind-blowing numbers in the chart on page 5. Government spending over the past 14 years has nearly doubled, from less than $1.3 trillion per year to $2.3 trillion. It suggests that Congress seems to consider it un-American to pass a yearly budget smaller than the one before it. In fact, government spending has not declined from any year to the next in the past half-century.

The $2.3 trillion the federal government will fork out this year exceeds the revenues it will have in its coffers by more than $500 billion—and that doesn't even count the cost of the continuing occupation of Iraq, which President Bush did not include in his official budget and which could add an additional $50 billion to $70 billion or more to the deficit.

To get an idea of the magnitude of a number the size of 2.3 trillion, consider this: If you tried to count to just one trillion at a rate of one number per second, it would take you 31,688 years. Put another way, a trillion seconds ago, Neanderthals were wandering the plains of Europe.

To be sure, two wars, a stock market crash, a recession—all have battered the budget in recent years. But make no mistake, the lion's share of the problem comes from relentless spending, made worse by big tax cuts aimed primarily at rich people. Last year alone, the government lost $242 billion of revenues to Bush's tax cuts, with the majority of the savings going to the wealthiest 1 percent of Americans. (Bush's own cut totaled $30,858.) The lost revenue could have significantly reduced the federal budget deficit. Instead, the tax cuts forced the Treasury to borrow more for running the government. This boosted the national debt, requiring extra interest payments to lenders. Put another way, last year's $242 billion favor for roughly 2.9 million Americans ultimately cost the other 290 million Americans some $256.7 billion, according to the nonpartisan Citizens for Tax Justice. Over the next decade, the total hit from those tax cuts will rise to $3.3 trillion if all of them are made permanent, as the President proposes.

Magnifying the budget damage wrought by tax cuts are this Administration's and Congress's undisciplined spending habits. In just two years, President Bush and the Republican-controlled Congress produced a 24 percent increase in discretionary spending, the biggest jump since World War II. This is 24 times the comparable number during the Clinton years. And, again, the current figure for discretionary spending doesn't include the ongoing cost of occupying Iraq.

Conservative economist Milton Friedman had it exactly right when he remarked not long ago: "What really matters is spending." Senator John McCain, one of the GOP's few visible wits, doesn't disagree. But in likening his party's big spenders to sailors on a binge, McCain wryly notes that "drunken sailors at least spend their own money."

- **WE'RE BORROWING TOO MUCH.**

Meet the mother of all scary numbers: $7,300,000,000,000. That's where the national debt hovers today on its fastest, steepest climb

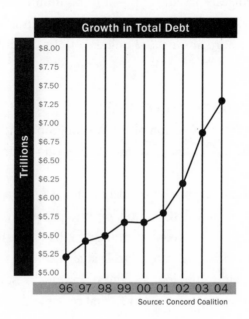

Growth in Total Debt

Source: Concord Coalition

since World War II (see the chart on page 7). And it's increasing by half a trillion dollars a year.

This colossus of borrowed cash is a monument to our leaders' shameless fiscal behavior. It dangles over us like a giant sword of Damocles, threatening to lop off America's future.

In 2000, the national debt was $5.7 trillion—a number that failed to alarm only because it eluded understanding (at one second per number, it would take 180,746 years to count). But then came the George W. Bush era. In three years, the debt has risen more than 25 percent. It is exploding, and no one in charge seems to be saying enough is enough. Congress keeps raising the debt limit, which, along with increasing spending, seems to be that august body's principal function.

Here's what the biggest national debt in the history of the world means to you personally. On September 30, 2003, the end of the federal government's fiscal year, each American family's share of what was then a $6.78 trillion debt (you can see how fast the debt grows) stood at $91,259. But not for long. Just since September 30, the debt has ballooned at an average rate of $1.4 billion every day. Unless something changes, that adds up—at a minimum—to another $511 billion a year, or nearly $7,000 more per American family, dumping an ever heavier burden on the shoulders of our children and grandchildren.

• **INTEREST RATES COULD KILL US.**
The most astonishing delusion of the Washington mind is that federal cash is limitless. In fact, the government lives on plastic and burgeoning debt.

Last year alone, interest on the debt claimed $318 billion of government revenues. To put that $318 billion into perspective, it accounted for 17 percent of our budgeted spending. If it had gone toward providing the country with something of real value, it could have paid for veterans' benefits, aid to the jobless, education initiatives, environmental protection, our space program, our federal courts and law enforcement,

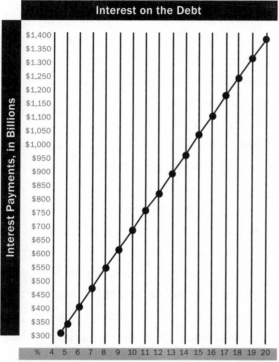

Source: Calculated by the author using data from the Bureau of Public Debt

and the Departments of Commerce, Interior, Energy, and State, plus international aid—with billions of dollars left over.

Instead, those dollars were thrown away as ransom for reckless fiscal policies of the past and present, things like those massive tax cuts and the second-lowest level of corporate income tax revenues since the Great Depression. In fact, 60 percent of U.S. corporations paid no tax at all last year. The revenue lost through Bush's tax cuts for business totaled $44 billion in fiscal 2002, $53 billion in 2003, and is projected to reach $64 billion this fiscal year—not one cent of which has been offset by spending cuts elsewhere.

Today's interest rates are at 46-year lows; they have nowhere to go but up. (Despite what you may have read, the Federal Reserve Board can't control them completely.) Even if by some miracle we never borrowed another nickel and quit adding more than $1 billion every day to the national debt, a rise in interest rates to the double-digit levels last seen in 1981, little more than two decades ago, would cause the payments on our current debt to consume every dollar of the government's tax revenues. There would be no money left to spend on anything else, from defense to Social Security to government salaries.

The more government spends, the more it has to borrow; the more it borrows, the more it has to spend for interest on its loans. Last year's $318 billion in interest on the national debt meant that we paid an average 4.6 percent. At 9 percent interest, we would pay roughly twice as much ($636 billion), leaving too little cash on hand to cover Social Security, Medicare, and Medicaid beneficiaries—and nothing to pay for nondefense discretionary programs such as education, justice, transportation, and other government functions we take for granted. The inevitable shortfalls would, of course, require still more borrowing and still more interest payments, ballooning the debt even more.

You get the picture: If interest rates climb and tax rates don't keep up, then at some point the government's interest payments will exceed its tax revenues. And that assumes that the debt isn't constantly expanding, which it is. The chart on the previous page shows the rising-interest path to fiscal collapse. At last year's income tax revenues of $1.3 trillion, total insolvency would occur when rates hit 18 percent, thereby pushing interest costs above total tax revenues. And if you think 18 percent interest rates are out of the question, think again. We surpassed that number in the early 1980s, a decade that many of us remember all too well.

To put it bluntly, this country is facing national insolvency in the near future. Interest rates on Treasury securities are at historic lows. And when they go up, as they most assuredly will, paying those rates will consume more and more of the government's income.

For every bump higher in interest rates, we will have to come up with more cash for our creditors—and the choices will be grim: We can either increase our overall debt and borrow more to finance it, risk recession by sharply boosting tax rates, or squeeze money out of desirable federal programs like Head Start for underprivileged children, benefits for the unemployed, or support for wounded veterans.

As the chart on page 9 vividly illustrates, unless we take drastic steps to halt our continuing budget deficits, we simply won't have enough revenue coming in to cover borrowing costs. Suddenly, the tidal wave of debt will swamp us, ending our ability to meet our obligations.

When that happens, America the beautiful will become America the broke.

Before that black day arrives, we can expect a series of frightening events caused by the government's insatiable spending spree and consequent need to borrow money. Interest rates will surely soar (hurting everyone, not just Uncle Sam). The government is not immune to the laws of supply and demand, and the more it borrows, the more its lenders will charge. This will force the Treasury to print more dollars, accelerating a plunge in the value of our currency (it has already fallen 30 percent against the euro in the last two years). How our lenders react will then depend a great deal on who and where they are.

- **WE DEPEND ON FOREIGNERS TO KEEP US AFLOAT.**

If you thought the only deficit we had to worry about is the one our leaders in Washington have been adding to every year, I've got more

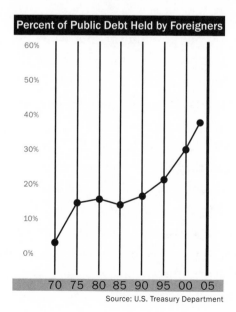

Source: U.S. Treasury Department

bad news for you. We have a serious trade deficit problem. We import far more goods than we export.

Thanks to our huge and growing appetite for goods from abroad—such as our burgeoning dependence on foreign oil—last year's trade deficit reached a record $489 billion. In other words, foreigners ended up holding that many dollars more than they sent back to us in payment for the American goods they purchased.

Dollars are basically not spendable anywhere but here. Accordingly, the foreign holders used a sizable portion of their dollars to buy our Treasury securities. Put another way, they lent us back a large share of the dollars we paid them for their imports. Sound good? Not quite. Trouble is, we now owe approximately 40 percent of our publicly held national debt to foreign interests.

It's still true that he who pays the piper calls the tune; in other words, our destiny is increasingly controlled by foreign hands. They will tolerate our excesses only so long as it suits their purposes, which may or may not coincide with ours.

Let's suppose these investors grow worried about the rising flood of U.S. debt securities and the government's ability to pay interest on its massive debt. As a result of what they perceive as increased risk, they may well demand higher rent (aka interest) for letting us borrow their money to run our government. But when interest rates jump, boosting the cost of borrowing, the government is forced to take a bigger bite out of already insufficient revenues. The shortfall raises the budget deficit even more, thereby pushing interest rates still higher. And so the vicious cycle continues.

Foreign investors are more likely than domestic ones to insist on higher rates because they already take on an additional risk when they buy our Treasury bonds: If the dollar declines in value before they cash out their bonds, they will receive less when they convert the dollars into their home currency. And guess what? The dollar has been steadily declining in recent years. Remember, it lost 30 percent of its value against the euro in 2002 and 2003 alone, which means that a European holder cashing in a fixed-rate two-year U.S. bond took a 30 percent hit in terms of the euros he could buy with his dollars.

Because foreign investors view the dollar as nothing more than another asset they buy in hopes of making a return, increasing economic turmoil in the United States would probably provoke them to sell some, if not all, of their dollar assets, causing the currency's value to drop farther. As this vicious cycle gathered speed, foreign investors might quit buying Treasury securities altogether. They might even start cashing in the bonds they already held. That would force the government to print the money it couldn't borrow—a surefire trigger for inflation and another blow to the value of the dollar.

What would happen then? We can only guess, because such a debacle has never occurred in modern times. At the very least, the United States—and because of our wide-ranging influence, the rest of the world, too—would be plunged into economic chaos, all because of our unwillingness to rein in our reckless spending.

Being so beholden to foreign interests has other disadvantages as well. Common sense tells you that, as in the game of Monopoly, the players holding the most cash have the upper hand. For all our boasts about being the world's only superpower, our words carry less and less clout as our economic position weakens. Great Britain learned this humiliating lesson early in the last century, when its empire was in decline.

What is more, our unilateral foreign policies have made America increasingly unpopular among our traditional allies. A poll last year by the Pew Research Center, which surveyed 16,000 people in 20 countries, found deep dislike and outright fear of the United States in country after country—and not just in Muslim nations. Distrust and suspicion of our motives as a result of our war in Iraq extended to our allies in Asia, South America, and Europe. History suggests that if the world's disapproval intensifies enough, creditor nations will not hesitate to remind us who's holding the purse. Given that distrust and even hatred of the United States seem to be escalating, it's no great stretch to imagine our Asian, European, or Middle Eastern lenders threatening, however diplomatically, to turn off the cash spigot unless we heed their countries' wishes on some controversial economic or political issue. It might be tariffs, say, or disputes over trade rules—

matters that we mistakenly thought we could control simply because we are the world's superpower.

Hints of this worrisome subtext have already surfaced in the refusal by our traditional allies to pay a significant share of the costs of the war in Iraq, and in the European Community's chastening rebuffs of U.S.-based megacompanies, including General Motors and Microsoft. The tone is bound to become significantly harsher as the scenario of default plays out.

• **THE DEBT CRISIS ISN'T JUST A GOVERNMENT PROBLEM. AMERICANS THEMSELVES FACE GREAT RISK BECAUSE MILLIONS OF US ARE SWIMMING IN PERSONAL DEBT.**

We're in hock for a record $2 trillion of consumer debt. That includes bank loans, car financing, and credit-card debt. Real-estate-related borrowing adds another $7 trillion. In less than 50 years, we've quit being a frugal people who once repaired, rebuilt, reused, and saved till we could afford to buy. Now we shun saving, worship novelty, shop till we drop, and raise kids to expect instant gratification. Result: unprecedented levels of consumer debt and personal bankruptcies—

Borrowing Binge

Billions	1993	1994	1995	1996	1997	1998	1999	2000	2001	2002	2003	2004
	809,325.43	872,021.82	1,010,217.43	1,149,767.24	1,253,980.62	1,310,217.52	1,420,510.90	1,528,367.69	1,702,946.79	1,828,402.94	1,915,193.25	2,014,351.08

Source: Federal Reserve Board, Historical Tables

1.6 million households filed papers last year alone. If we can't get smart about our personal finances, how can we cope with the government's follies?

For the first time in history, Americans owe more than they take home in after-tax income. Personal debt is now three times bigger than the gross domestic product. Credit-card debt alone averages about $8,000 per household, another all-time high. Whose credit-card debt is rising the fastest? The answer may surprise you: senior citizens'.

Moreover, those paying the most for credit are the people who can least afford it. If you spread the credit-card debt only among families who don't pay up before financing charges kick in, it's more like $12,000 per household. Fees rise sharply, to an annual rate as high as 24 percent, at the first delinquency or even late payment. All told, about 25 percent of low-income Americans spend at least 40 percent or more of their earnings just to pay interest on their existing debt. How will these people escape their constantly increasing debt? What happens to their finances as credit-card interest rates rise?

As if credit-card debt weren't enough, we've had sharp increases (averaging 27.5 percent) since 2001 in mortgage borrowing, home equity loans, and the like. The mortgage-refinance boom that swept America in recent years, as interest rates fell to 46-year lows, tempted many homeowners to take cash payments when they refinanced, siphoning off some of their built-up equity. They used the cash they netted to pay down other debt, buy cars or other consumer goods, take vacations, or spiff up their homes. Unfortunately, they now have less equity in their homes—equity levels have fallen to 56 percent of the value of the home, on average—than ever before. Their mortgage providers talked up the virtues of *adjustable* interest rates—rates that seemed low then but could become crippling when (not if) interest costs shoot up again.

DENYING THE SITUATION

Yet the incumbents running for reelection loudly deny that anything is wrong. We have now reached Condition Red on the denial chart.

Most politicians hunger first and foremost to be reelected. Why? I'd like to tell you that it's so they can nobly serve their country. But their behavior suggests it's so they can continue to guzzle ignobly at the public trough. By their deeds, so at odds with their words, we can only conclude that they yearn to hang on and on in Washington, spending ever more tax dollars on special interests that return the favor by financing the politicians' reelection campaigns. And when they finally retire on hefty government pensions, they report for duty as fat-cat lobbyists, selling government access to the highest bidders. This is fiscal felony. A quicker way to spend the republic into insolvency is hard to imagine. Mark Twain cut to the bone in the 1890s when he wrote, "There is no distinctly native American criminal class, except Congress."

The only thing that's changed since Twain's time is the undreamt size of the national debt riding on American backs and budgets. Whatever happened to fiduciary responsibility? In Washington, that quaint term is used only to pull the wool over our eyes, the way a con man says "Trust me" before he steals you blind.

"Deficits don't matter," purr Vice President Dick Cheney and other members of the Bush Administration, as well as our U.S. senators and representatives who control the national checkbook. Whatever they claim, whatever deceits our elected officials spin to hide fiscal fecklessness from naïve voters, I am here to tell you that the huge tabs they're running up in our name, both at home and abroad, *do* matter. These numbers don't lie. America's supposed economic juggernaut is already dangling over a chasm, and the rope belaying us is fast unraveling. Nearly everything we take for granted—democracy itself—is under siege.

This looming crisis didn't spring up overnight. It is the product of years of false assumptions, misguided policies, and partisan politics—in some cases, downright despicable behavior—by our presidents and Congress, past and present. In the chapters that follow, I'll show you what's gone on and why we now face a potentially catastrophic threat to our way of life.

It is not my intent to exaggerate that threat, but I sense that even the shocking facts I will relate may not fully convey the grave danger I'm convinced we face. Sometimes it takes a jolt of imagination to visualize what such insolvency might mean. The next chapter paints a frightening picture of how the coming collapse—a sudden switch from abundance and liberty to poverty and bondage—might look and feel to a typical American family—a family that could well be your own.

CHAPTER 2

DEPENDENCE DAY

THEY SAID IT couldn't happen here. Not in the richest, safest nation on earth. Not where prosperity shines, the dollar reigns, and opportunity beckons. But they were wrong—the apologists, the politicians, the liars. Dead wrong. Suddenly, and seemingly out of nowhere, the U.S. economy was ripped apart by a surprise attack that undermined millions of lives and destroyed billions of dollars of assets.

With the power of a hundred hurricanes, insolvency raged across the land, crippling the federal government, leveling corporations, and sweeping away much of the middle class as prosperous people became paupers overnight.

It was the bleakest week in American history, a calamity that scholars would take decades to sort out. As in my earlier book, *Bankruptcy 1995*, this chapter is devoted to illustrating the devastating impact of the crisis on one American family. It shows how the crisis might play out for two typical middle-class Americans, Alice and Bill Ringer, once modestly affluent baby boomers living in a Chicago suburb.

SUNDAY

It was just after one o'clock on Sunday morning when the jangle of their bedside phone woke Bill and Alice. A nurse at the hospital was calling with—what else at one o'clock in the morning?—bad news: Jeffrey, the Ringers' 18-year-old son, had been injured in a freak accident. His car fell 20 feet onto the interstate highway, along with tons of rubble, when the Maple Avenue overpass collapsed. The nurse said Jeffrey had a concussion but would survive. A passerby, however, hadn't been so lucky—he was dead.

"We knew that overpass was in bad shape," Bill cried, tears running down his face as he pulled his sweater over his head. "Why didn't they pass that bond issue last year? It could have been replaced."

There wasn't much the Ringers could do at the hospital. Jeffrey was sedated, looking pale and bruised, and he wouldn't wake until afternoon. So Alice and Bill went home to try to get some sleep. They had planned to get up early to help Alice's parents move out of their house and into the Ringers' guest bedroom.

Alice's parents, Bob and Maude Adams, had lived in their modest brick house for 54 years, raising five children, living a full and happy life. They had long since paid off the mortgage and burned it ceremoniously at a big party to mark the occasion. But the Adamses had been devastated by the stock market disaster three years ago. Bob had put most of his savings into high-tech stocks, which doubled in value. Then the bubble began to deflate, and Bob seemed helpless to sell off his remaining assets as his portfolio tumbled 80 percent.

The Adamses had struggled along for a couple of years on Bob's railroad pension, but recently his pension had been slashed because the railroad pension funds had lost too much. Now the debts were running up. It was only when Bill suggested they could take a reverse mortgage on their house that Bob finally confessed to borrowing against the house's value to cover their living costs. Less than $100,000 of equity was left. When a reassessment threatened to double the Adamses' tax bill, they had no alternative but to sell.

The previous evening, the Ringers had stayed up late worrying about the turn their lives were taking. Alice's parents had gotten a fair price for the house; it just happened that Lucky Goldstar, the Korean electronics giant, was putting together a big parcel of land on which to build a huge new automated warehouse—a place that would handle hundreds of millions of dollars' worth of parts. But, Bill groused, it would probably support fewer than a hundred jobs. At this rate, it wouldn't be long before no one would be able to buy the company's damned cell phones, because no one would have a pay-ing job.

Bill himself had been forced to put off buying a new car a month ago. He had had his eye on a Ford truck that listed for around $25,000 but got a shock when he saw the size of the payments. Three years ago, he could have bought the truck with zero-percent financ-ing. Today, the loan rate was 10 percent, which added $200 worth of interest to the monthly payment. Bill couldn't swing it. Plenty of other buyers must have felt the same way. He had read recently that all the auto companies were laying off workers and cutting production.

The salesman told him the jump in interest rates had something to do with the national debt. Bill had spent hours on the Internet exploring sites that might explain the connection. Last night, over coffee in the family room, he tried to describe to Alice what the economists said about how the high loan payments, the loss of auto-manufacturing jobs, and the plunge in her father's pension fund and in the value of her parents' house were all connected to the expanding federal debt and deficit. The national debt had ballooned to frighten-ing levels, yet the politicians continued to claim that deficits didn't matter.

"I never did understand how the government could afford such a huge debt," Alice said, as she sat straight up in her chair, the light behind her making a sort of halo around her light brown hair. "If we had that kind of debt, we'd be bankrupt."

Bill smiled wanly at her, running his fingers through his hair. "I know. The politicians kept claiming government finances weren't like our family budget," he said. But maybe the politicians were wrong, he explained. The federal budget, which briefly ran a surplus six years ago, had been deep in the red ever since. New entitlement programs such as the Medicare drug benefit—with a $500 billion price tag over 10 years (and that was probably a lowball guesstimate)—had dramatically ratcheted up expenditures. The institutions and foreigners lending the U.S. government money to finance the national debt started insisting on a higher rate of interest to make up for the added risk. Foreign lenders were especially skittish.

"Added risk?" Alice repeated, and Bill said, "Well, there's a small risk that the investors won't get repaid at all. But the real risk is that the government will print more money to make it easier to pay off the debt. That would devalue the currency, so when the investors get their money back, it won't be worth as much." It had happened before in the 1970s and 1980s, he explained. Even after inflation was brought under control, rates stayed high for years while the lenders made up their losses.

Short-term interest rates three years ago were less than 1 percent, Bill reminded Alice. Now they were edging up to 3 percent, and 10-year Treasury bonds were paying 6 percent. That level used to be considered normal, but having to apply that rate to a national debt now well over $9 trillion was devastating. It was costing the government an extra $500 billion just to service the debt this year, lifting the federal government's annual budget deficit to almost $1 trillion.

The rising costs of borrowing by the government pushed up interest rates across the board. "And that's why we can't afford the new truck," Bill said. Alice realized that other people she knew were having similar problems. Her boss had been planning to expand his fast-growing digital-animation company, but financing got so expensive that he had to postpone his plans. The financial-advice columns said the no-jobs recovery had dragged the economy back into recession. The stock market had taken another severe hit, and the real-estate bubble that seemed a permanent fixture just a few years ago had finally popped, with prices rapidly collapsing. "That has hurt your dad's pension, too," Bill said. "His union's fund put way too much money into growth stocks and real estate. That's why Bob had to take a pension cut."

It was midnight before Alice and Bill finished talking. They had barely fallen into bed and asleep when the hospital called. By the time they saw Jeffrey at the hospital and returned home, it was nearly 5 A.M. It was no surprise that their eyes felt gritty when they got up again two hours later.

The rest of Sunday went by in a blur—a quick visit to Jeffrey in the hospital was sandwiched between trips to Alice's childhood home, which was strangely bare of furniture. Alice and Bill lugged carloads of the Adamses' belongings up to their attic or down to the basement. Proud of his roomy, colonial-style house and its neatly landscaped lot, Bill resented the clutter he was creating, but he knew there was no other choice.

Finally, Bob and Maude were settled in the guest room, apologizing at every turn for the bother they were causing. Alice knew it was going to be hard for everyone to adjust. Luckily, her daughter Erica was away at college, but still the house felt crowded and uncomfortable with the addition of her parents. But what else could they do?

MONDAY

Alice's mother fixed breakfast Monday morning, allowing Alice to get to work a few minutes early. The office manager at the digital-animation company, Alice also worked in personnel and in receivables. It seemed as if every one of the 14 employees did more than one job. With sales doubling every six months and new customers coming onboard almost daily, there was always too much to do.

As Alice sorted through the day's schedule, an instant message popped up on her computer screen asking everyone to meet in the conference room at 10 A.M. Alice finished her coffee and walked down the hall.

"Good morning," said Michael Robinson, the company's young founder, to his assembled staff. Uncharacteristically, he seemed to be groping for words, nervously fiddling with his glasses. "I'm sorry," he finally said. "You're wonderful people, and you've done a fine job. But at the end of the week, this company will be out of business."

There was a stunned silence. How could this be? Customers were pouring in, and there was more work than the staff could handle. Michael explained that receivables were outrunning the company's cash flow; customers were taking so long to pay their bills that he didn't have enough cash to meet his expenses. The company had a line of credit with the bank for just this reason, and there had never been any question about its ability to make loan payments. Just six months ago, in fact, the bank had discussed providing another loan to finance an expansion of the business. But now the bank's officers had told Michael they were canceling the credit line on orders from state regulators to reduce the bank's overall level of risk and rebuild its capital base. And the venture capitalists who initially bankrolled Michael's company had rejected his latest plea for cash, claiming that they, too, were overextended.

Michael said he had tried and failed to find a buyer for the company and now was looking for buyers for some of his product lines. A Japanese company might purchase the inventory-control software line, he said, and might even hire some of the staff, but he could make no promises. Everyone would be paid through the end of the month.

Alice was bewildered. She loved her job, the people, and the sheer excitement of being part of a thriving enterprise. And she needed the salary. The Ringer family's finances depended on it.

That night at the dinner table, talk was strained. Bill was silent, trying to digest the shock of Alice's being laid off. Bob and Maude were still mourning their house, and Alice didn't want to tell them her bad news on top of everything else.

The one blessing was that Jeffrey was home from the hospital; his emotional account of the accident gave them something to focus on. His cell phone had saved him, he said. The car was almost buried in the debris from the collapsed overpass, but he reached the 911 operator, who guided the rescuers to him. His eyes welled with tears at the thought of the death of the pedestrian on the overpass.

The Adamses went to bed early. Alice and Bill sat in the family room trying to figure out what to do next. Alice made a list of her contacts in other high-tech businesses. She planned to start calling them in the morning.

Bill told her the credit-card companies were all raising their monthly rates. Until Alice found a new job, they might have to cut back the monthly payment on their credit-card debt, paying just the minimum demanded by the company. If they kept that up for long, Bill thought, they would be so deep in the hole they'd never get out. Bill also knew that the anniversary of their adjustable mortgage was coming up. The interest rate he paid would surely be adjusted upward by the maximum two percentage points permitted annually. He shuddered to think how much extra per month that would cost them, and he cursed himself for not having chosen the fixed rate of 5 percent when he refinanced back in 2003. He didn't even want to remember that they had used part of their home equity to take a vacation in Mexico.

All in all, it seemed wise to cut their spending to the bone, Bill and Alice decided. They would stay at home for vacation this year and hold off on buying the new dining-room furniture they were considering. Of course, if everyone in the same boat followed suit, Bill reflected, it could cause a recession that would hurt every American. But what choice did they have?

TUESDAY

While Bill was driving to work Tuesday morning, he heard on the radio that Congress was still deadlocked over the federal deficit. As rising interest rates ate up more of the government's revenues just to pay the interest on the debt, the deficit was expanding and pushing out nearly all discretionary spending, the newscaster said. To narrow the gap between revenues and spending, some lawmakers wanted budget cuts, others wanted higher taxes. But the only measure everyone could agree on was the administration's energy bill. It sailed through both houses of Congress with earmarked pieces of pork attached for the states and districts of every senator and representative who supported the bill, adding to the government's expenditures.

Bill was a vice president at a small machine-tool company that made sophisticated manufacturing equipment, largely for the auto industry and a few defense contractors. His plant was a rambling old factory in the industrial section of Chicago.

An engineer, Bill enjoyed the challenge of building specialized high-speed lathes, routers, metal-forming presses, and the like to handle new manufacturing tasks. Today, though, he learned that a customer had unexpectedly canceled the job he was working on. Bill had to put his crew on routine maintenance and set up for a new job. That meant an easy day and probably an easy week, but Bill was worried. He had never seen an order canceled so abruptly in midproduction. Quietly, he asked company president Lowell Banks what it meant. Nothing good, said Lowell, but he wouldn't say anything more. Lowell seemed to tell his people less than ever since a big conglomerate bought the company last year.

That night, while Alice and Maude were cleaning up the dinner dishes, Alice suddenly wondered how they could keep Erica in the state university next year. The papers were reporting that a big tuition jump was soon to be announced because interest costs were overburdening the state education system. Well, she reflected wryly, by next year the family would surely qualify for a lot more scholarship aid—that is, if the school had any to pass out.

WEDNESDAY

Wednesday was an eerie, anxious day at work for Bill. Lowell Banks spent the day in his office with the door closed, apparently on the phone most of the time. The machine operators were aimlessly reprogramming their equipment, listening to the news on the radio.

Bill got on his computer and started surfing the Internet. He went to *The New York Times*'s Web site and found an article that explained the situation that had killed off Alice's company. U.S. banks were in a squeeze, the account said. For years, they made long-term loans at low rates. But now their depositors were demanding higher rates: The banks were having to pay customers as much as 10 percent on six-month certificates of deposit. The 5 percent fixed rates paid by mortgage borrowers weren't going to cover the banks' costs. They had to foreclose or call in every note they could.

Another article reported that interest rates in money markets were spiking up to levels that hadn't been seen in 25 years. Foreign investors, once a major source of loans for the U.S. government, were beginning to cut their losses and run for the exits. In the bond market, as the article explained, bond prices fall as interest rates rise, so in order to unload their bonds and notes, the foreign investors had had to cut their asking prices until short-term interest rates soared to 10 percent—10 times higher than a year ago. The rate on the 10-year Treasury bond jumped to 16 percent, fully four times what it had yielded in 2003.

All signs were now pointing to the rapid growth of inflation, which would eat into the dollar's value against other currencies. To Bill, it was clear that foreigners investing in U.S. government bonds today faced a double whammy: Not only would their bonds lose value as interest rates rose, but when the bonds were sold, the holder would be repaid in devalued dollars that would buy fewer euros or yen. So, naturally, foreigners wouldn't buy dollars unless they were heavily discounted. The dollar, which had been sinking slowly on world markets ever since 2001, was now plunging.

On the drive home, Bill heard on the radio that the chaos in the money markets had finally scared Congress into breaking the deadlock over the deficit; they were enacting emergency cost cuts. "Defying major pressure by the AARP and other senior groups," the announcer said, "an emergency joint committee of Congress voted today to cut Social Security payments by 20 percent and to delay the retirement age to 72." The announcer went on to say that the President was promising the Social Security cutbacks would be temporary. The news hit Bill like a punch in the stomach. What would happen to Alice's parents? Would the government revoke benefits for people already receiving them? What about his own retirement, just 10 years away?

News of the Social Security cuts had intensified the sell-off on Wall Street. The Dow closed at 6,520, off 225 points for the week so far. The market had lost more than 4,000 points from its peak in early 2004, but some analysts thought the worst was still to come. Thinking of his 401(k) retirement savings plan, Bill cursed. Where once he had nearly $100,000 socked away, growing in a tax-free account, he now had less than $60,000.

When Bill got home, Alice told him her own disturbing news: A run of panicky customers at the local bank had tried to withdraw their deposits just before closing time. "I'm going down there tomorrow," Alice said. Bill pointed out that all deposits were federally insured up to $100,000, but he didn't really try to talk her out of it.

THURSDAY

It was rare to see financial news outside the business pages of the *Chicago Tribune*, but on Thursday Alice found a story on page one.

"U.S. ALLIES SLAM DOLLAR," the headline blared. The article went on to say that central bankers in Japan, China, and Europe, worried about inflation in their own countries, would stop intervening to support the American dollar in currency trading, letting it fall as it would. In a biting joint statement, Britain, Germany, France, and Japan assailed Washington for its "irresponsible fiscal policies" and said they could no longer accept its promises of future spending restraint. After the announcement, a massive sell-off drove down the price of the dollar relative to other currencies around the world.

Alice asked Bill, "Exactly what does this mean for us?" "For one thing," Bill said, "the price of Mexican tomatoes and French wine will probably go up, and we won't be taking any trips to Italy."

Alice put the morning's news out of her mind as she left for the office. Although the company was shutting down tomorrow, many tasks still needed attention, and it wasn't in her nature to leave the place in a mess. When she arrived, she was surprised at the number of people who had shown up. Most were working the phones, looking for jobs. Alice did a bit of calling, too, but all she got was sympathy.

Betsy, who worked just down the hall, told Alice that her father was at risk of losing a big chunk of his retirement benefits. He'd been drawing $514 a month from his company's pension fund, but severe losses in the value of the fund's bond investments resulted in liabilities that now outweighed its assets. So the company was turning its fund over to the federal Pension Benefit Guarantee Corporation (PBGC). The problem was that the federal plan didn't have enough money to handle all the pension funds that were going broke. As a result, the monthly payment to Betsy's father was going to be chopped in half. "How awful," Alice said. She didn't tell Betsy that her own father might well be in the same boat.

Alice pulled up to the Cook County Savings Bank just after noon and found a crowd gathered outside. A bystander told her the bank was closed. He said several government banking agents had driven up and announced that the bank was no longer in business. "They told us not to worry, that our money is government insured. But how long will it take to collect it?" he wondered out loud. Alice opened her purse to find just $57. That won't go far, she thought in a panic. Well, there's always the credit cards and the checking account.

But what if the checking account didn't work either? Alice almost ran to the nearest ATM. A dozen people waited in line to use it. As she watched, some got cash, others got only slips of white paper. Apparently, some banks were giving out money, others weren't. When Alice got to the machine, she entered her PIN, then hesitated. Then she boldly punched in a withdrawal of $500, five times her usual amount. "SORRY," the screen read, "WITHDRAWALS ARE LIMITED TO $100 AT THIS TIME. THANK YOU FOR YOUR PATIENCE AND UNDERSTANDING." Alice hit the $100 fast-cash button, took the money, and tried to do it again. "YOU HAVE JUST WITH-DRAWN THE MAXIMUM," the screen told her. Feeling irrationally guilty for having tried to withdraw her own money, she put the bills in her purse and headed off to the supermarket to shop for dinner.

Meat seemed to be in short supply at the store, and what was there was both pricey and unappealing. Alice bought pasta instead, and some of Bill's favorite Alfredo sauce, frozen peas, and the makings of a salad. Though she was buying enough for five people, Alice was shocked at the cash register when the total came to more than $30. The two jars of pasta sauce cost nearly $17 and the head of lettuce $4.99, while the frozen peas had gone up to $2.75 and the box of spaghetti that used to cost $1.99 was now a whopping $5.99! Well, sure, it's from Italy, she thought. But it didn't come over this week. This is just profiteering. She took the stuff back to the shelf and bought American brands instead.

Bill spent another empty day at the plant, surfing for news and worrying. He caught Lowell Banks coming out of his office, but learned only that there would be an announcement of some sort tomorrow. Lowell wouldn't say what it was. At lunchtime, Bill tried to get cash from an ATM, but, like Alice, he could withdraw only $100. The amount suddenly seemed inadequate, so he dropped in at the bank. Don Howard, one of the vice presidents with whom Bill sometimes played golf, agreed to help Bill out. Mumbling that he wasn't supposed to be doing this, Don initialed Bill's check to withdraw $500. When the teller gave him the money, Bill briefly felt a bit better.

When Bill got home, the pasta sauce bubbling on the stove smelled delicious, but the pleasant sensation he experienced soon evaporated with the evening news. The U.S. Treasury auction this morning had been a disaster. Too few bids for the government bonds and notes left half of the offering unsold, even at sharply higher interest rates. Maturing notes were coming due Friday, but today's half-sold offering meant the government wouldn't have the funds needed for repayment. The financial markets were in turmoil. The stock market had closed an hour early, at 3 P.M., with the Dow off more than 500 points, one of its worst days in recent memory. A senior senator, who wished to remain anonymous, was quoted as saying: "Today, our country has become the Weimar Republic." Subsequent interviews with bankers, stock traders, homemakers, and supermarket managers revealed that everyone was worried. Bill abruptly turned off the TV, and the family sat down to dinner in silence.

FRIDAY

"CRISIS EASES," read the headline in Friday morning's paper. The Federal Reserve Board, meeting in emergency session Thursday night, had agreed to pump billions of dollars into the economy by buying up the notes and bonds that went unsold in yesterday's auction. It was a stopgap measure designed to calm the markets and provide a little breathing space. But the Federal Reserve chairman and the secretary of the Treasury agreed that the nation's finances were basically sound. They said there was no cause for alarm. The infusion of funds, the chairman said, would be enough for the banks to meet any short-term cash-flow problems. He added that the system should be back on track by Monday.

Driving to the plant, Bill felt slightly better—until he tuned in to a morning talk show. The guest on this morning's program was a banker, who said: "Gene, I tell you, it's textbook inflation. They make it sound good, but what the Federal Reserve Board did was print money, pure and simple. They bought those bonds with rubber checks. What it means is that everyone's money is worth that much less this morning."

The country was headed for insolvency, the host agreed, just as the International Monetary Fund had warned early in 2004. It was rumored that the United States Mint planned to bring back the $1,000 bill, which hadn't been printed since 1934. Were $50,000 and $100,000 bills far behind? Bill's stomach was churning.

When he got to work, rumors were flying that their subsidiary's parent company was about to close the facility and move production to China. Twenty people out of 500 would keep their jobs. A plantwide meeting was called in the lathe production bay, the largest open space in the plant. As a vice president, Bill had to sit up front with the brass while the others squeezed into the gaps between machines. But he was just as stunned as everyone else to learn that the real news was worse than the rumors. The plant was indeed closing, Lowell Banks said. But all the remaining work would be outsourced—no one would have a job.

Someone shouted that the owners couldn't just lay them off like that—the law required two months' warning, or pay to match. Lowell Banks just shrugged, and Bill realized that in the nation's rapidly expanding crisis, legal quibbles would get short shrift. Lowell said final paychecks would be mailed out, and everyone should gather up his or her belongings in the locker room and leave now, without going back into the plant or offices. A squad of security guards filed into the lunchroom and started herding people toward the locker room. Some of them were cursing and shoving back. Others were crying.

As Bill stood up, one of the machine operators yelled at him: "Bill! Hell of a friend you turned out to be! Couldn't you at least have given us a warning?" Bill spread his hands helplessly, feeling ashamed. The guys wouldn't believe that he hadn't known beforehand. He couldn't believe it himself. Shoulders hunched, Bill walked quietly into the locker room.

At Alice's office, Michael called the staff into the conference room for a farewell drink just after lunch. Saying he wouldn't make a speech, Michael thanked them all for doing a fantastic job and wished them better luck in the future. "You'll all get top references from me, and if there's anything else I can do, I want you to tell me." Many people cried.

On her way home, Alice decided that it wouldn't hurt to stock up on basic supplies and enough groceries to last at least a week. But when she reached the supermarket, it was jammed with people who had the same idea—and the prices were even more mind-boggling than the day before. Meat was out of the question: A beef pot roast that ought to be $4.99 a pound was now nearly $15.00. Vermont cheddar cheese that she thought expensive at $5.99 a pound now had two stickers hiding that long-gone price; one said $7.99 and the top one read $10.99. Some things, like the fresh produce from South America and the lamb from New Zealand, weren't marked at all. Instead, a sign said: "Prices on request at the register." It was like shopping at Tiffany's, Alice thought.

She focused on staples and less expensive items, filling her cart with toilet paper, paper towels, dried beans and lentils, canned soups, cabbage, and root vegetables.

She got into the checkout line with only half of what she meant to get, then watched in shock as the bill mounted. It came to almost twice what she usually spent, in spite of forgoing meat and the priciest items. And when she presented her credit card, the checker said, "Is this credit? Sorry, only debit cards today." Alice dug in her purse and found her MasterCard debit card. But when the clerk swiped it through his machine, there was a beep. "Sorry," the woman said briskly. "This card's no good anymore." She whipped out a pair of scissors and cut it in half.

This couldn't be happening! Alice felt her mouth opening and closing, but no sound was coming out. Trying to make her feel better, the clerk said, "Don't worry, hon. It's not you, it's just the banks. The government will straighten it out."

In a daze, Alice abandoned the bagged groceries on the counter and stumbled out to her car. She suddenly thought that Bill would be upset with her for not demanding the pieces of her credit card, to prevent identity theft. They can have my identity, she thought. I don't want to be me anymore.

SATURDAY

It was Saturday morning, and Alice and Bill were pretending to sleep in. Bed was the only safe place to be, Bill joked weakly. He was a little hungover from too many beers last night. Angry, frustrated, and scared, he boiled over when Alice handed him the bill from the hospital for Jeffrey's tests and treatment. "Five thousand dollars and change," he yelled, "for one day in the hospital!" Worse yet, he had little hope that his company would make good on his medical benefits. Where was he supposed to get $5,000?

Lying in bed, the Ringers tried to sort out their situation. Both might receive their final paychecks—assuming, of course, that a bank would be open to cash them. They would register today for their meager unemployment benefits. Alice had her business skills and experience, and surely someone, somewhere would need her. Bill was an engineer and handy at fixing things. If he couldn't find a real job, he wasn't too proud to take menial work. In the early going, he might have just that much edge on the guys who looked down their noses at anything sweaty. Thanks to Don Howard at the bank, the Ringers had more than $600 in cash to tide them over until the banks reopened.

Bob Adams's pension, small as it was, would help out, and both he and Maude had their Social Security benefits (Bill hoped) and something left from the sale of their house, if they could get at the money.

A bit irrationally, perhaps, Bill somehow felt better. Facing up to the problems he knew about, and imagining what else could go wrong, made him less helpless, more in control, he thought. Taking stock, he told himself that he and Alice still had their health and each other. Besides that, they were tough people. Alice smiled at him, and he reached to hold her.

Once out of bed, Alice put on the coffee while Bill walked out into the yard, basking in the sun as he planned the spring cleanup. Next week has to be better, he thought. What could be worse? He leaned down to pick up the newspaper and read: "BANKS CLOSE. DOLLAR PLUMMETS. AMERICA IS BROKE, PRESIDENT SAYS."

CHAPTER 3

PROFILES IN COWARDICE

WHEN THE CALL came for something bigger than politics as usual, they didn't pick up the phone.

When the fiscal health of our country demanded healing action, they prescribed snake oil.

When the confluence of war and recession pleaded for sacrifice, they said, "Nonsense. We can borrow and spend with no thought for tomorrow."

Welcome to Profiles in Cowardice, the story of three decades of reckless fiscal behavior by a series of presidents and the men and women we elected to represent us in Congress, all of it brought to a head in the new millennium by the presidency of George W. Bush. With a chilling disregard for the consequences, Bush has jettisoned a workable bipartisan commitment reached during the presidency of Bill Clinton, a joint effort that had put us firmly on track to solving the nation's fiscal crisis. Instead, we are hurtling toward national insolvency on a wave of unrivaled deficit spending and unconscionable tax cuts that give the bulk of the savings to the richest members of our society.

How did America get to this point? How did we blindly stroll to the very edge of a national abyss, a bottomless pit that now threatens to swallow up Social Security, Medicare, Medicaid, support for the unemployed, and every remaining strand of the social and economic safety net we have woven since the Great Depression? How did we jeopardize our ability to pay for our national defense and the protection of our environment and every other governmental function we take for granted? How did we squander so much of the economic strength that underpins our position of power in the world?

Credit our leaders, the 535 Democrat and Republican members of Congress, their staffs and assistants, and the men we have elected president and those who have served under them. And credit us: Our leaders led the way, and we followed, often blindly. Dazzled by promises to provide a hand up to the less fortunate in our society and to extend medical benefits to all retirees, we failed to ask if we could really afford such generosity—or at least whether we should be offering it to everyone, regardless of financial status. Concerned about our ability to defend our very way of life in a dangerous world, we rarely questioned our leaders about the outrageously expensive costs of guns and gadgets and unproven missile defense systems. Our inattentiveness permitted boondoggles to flourish and spending to skyrocket.

It all began with good intentions. Until the last 40 years or so, the United States generally ran its financial house in a responsible manner. The rule was pay as you go: If added revenues were needed, taxes or tariffs were raised to provide them. Borrowings in time of war were reduced after the fighting ended, and the national debt shrank as a percentage of the gross domestic product. Even when President Franklin Delano Roosevelt followed the then-revolutionary economic theory of John Maynard Keynes, thereby generating huge deficits to fight the Depression and World War II, the return of peace and prosperity brought a return to balanced or nearly balanced budgets. In the course of its first 183 years, the United States accumulated a total debt of just $310 billion (the amount we now rack up in a matter of months).

But then Lyndon Johnson moved into the White House, opening a new and frightening chapter in our economic history. He and his successors have piled up deficit after deficit, presiding over a mounting fiscal calamity.

To be fair, our presidents have tried (at least until now) to restore some balance, to reconcile government spending with revenues. Most knew perfectly well that profligate spending could not continue forever. But there are always honest disagreements about national priorities, which inevitably trigger money disputes. Sometimes this leads to courageous but politically unpopular actions by presidents of either party (consider George H. W. Bush and Bill Clinton, both of whom raised taxes to counter rising deficits). More often, it leads to political expediency or shell-game accounting designed to mask shortfalls between spending and revenues.

Overall, it's a sorry record. Starting with LBJ, here's what our presidential wrecking crew has wrought. The dollar figures are those provided by each administration, but even these sanitized numbers can't hide our leaders' recklessness.

LYNDON JOHNSON

Fiscal discipline was ragged at best in the three-year presidency of John F. Kennedy, who recommended both spending increases to stimulate a sagging economy and tax cuts designed to restore confidence in the business community. But the fiscal discipline that existed was largely jettisoned on November 22, 1963, the day Kennedy's assassination thrust Lyndon B. Johnson into the White House. Johnson hoped to solve problems by throwing money at them. He planted the seeds of the present crisis by spending dollars he didn't have to fight a war

DEFICITS UNDER JOHNSON				
1964	1965	1966	1967	1968
−5.9	−1.4	−3.7	−8.6	−25.2

TOTAL DEFICIT 5 YEARS: $44.8 BILLION

against poverty at home and one against communism in Vietnam, without ever facing up to the true costs of either.

Knowing that he would be criticized for his fiscal irresponsibility, Johnson was determined to hide what he was doing and even tried to conceal the cost of the military buildup from his own top economists. He ordered the Pentagon to lowball cost estimates in confidential memos to the Council of Economic Advisers (CEA). The CEA officials were hardly fooled; council member Arthur Okun, who later became the CEA's chairman, scribbled on one such memo: "But not to be swallowed." Nonetheless, Johnson pushed his deceptive budgets through Congress, calling for only modest increases in the defense budget. In reality, military spending rose by an average of 18 percent for three straight years, from 1966 to 1968.

The country might have been able to absorb a wartime deficit, but runaway spending didn't end there. Johnson was simultaneously pouring what were then vast sums into his Great Society program, an ambitious effort to redeem the nation's promises to its less-fortunate citizens by ending poverty, promoting civil rights, improving education, and protecting the environment. The result of trying to have it all was a deficit that came to nearly $45 billion in the five years from 1964 through 1968, $25 billion of which was chalked up in 1968 alone. (Compare that $25 billion to 2004's projection of $500 billion of red ink and rising.)

Johnson's Great Society program achieved many of its goals and did much good, but at a heavy and unforeseen cost: It cemented into the federal budget what came to be known as entitlement programs, thus sending the budget spinning out of control.

In effect, an entitlement program decrees that anyone who fits a given profile has a right to receive government aid in the form of actual money or an equivalent such as food stamps. (Entitlement programs may also guarantee preferential treatment for jobs, housing, educational placement, and the like.) Before Johnson, only one major entitlement program existed and that was Social Security, which provides benefits to people of retirement age. LBJ's war on poverty added

Medicare, Medicaid, Aid to Families with Dependent Children, and college scholarship aid, among others—and spending on them has just kept growing.

Because entitlement benefits are automatic, they require no annual review or appropriation. And unless Congress musters the courage to try to curtail them, they are subject to neither vote nor veto. This means that spending on entitlement programs spirals constantly upward, with devastating side effects. First, the programs put a head-lock on fiscal policy, obliging the government to spend money whether it has it or not. They also make budget forecasting difficult, if not impossible, since no one knows how many people will show up for payment each year until they stop arriving. Worse yet, politicians can cynically "buy" votes by raising entitlement benefits or stretching them to cover new groups of voters. And any effort to cap benefits or cut them back naturally triggers a storm of protest. It's no wonder Social Security has been called the third rail of politics: Touch it and die.

So despite the acknowledged social progress fostered by Lyndon Johnson's vision of a Great Society, his economic legacy has been both destructive and lasting. The immediate punishment was a devastating inflation that Johnson's successors battled for more than a decade. But the long-term consequences were even more damaging. By encouraging the notion that deficit spending is permissible even when the nation's survival is not at stake, Johnson planted a land mine. It is this lethal menace, made ever more destructive by later administrations, that now threatens to explode in our faces.

RICHARD NIXON

President Richard M. Nixon was not the fiscal villain he is sometimes made out to be. To a large extent, he was the victim of a situation he inherited—and while federal spending bulged ominously for a while, the trend was in the right direction during the last two years of the Nixon Administration.

DEFICITS UNDER NIXON					
1969	1970	1971	1972	1973	1974
+3.2	-2.8	-23.0	-23.4	-14.9	-6.1

TOTAL DEFICIT 6 YEARS: $67.0 BILLION

When LBJ indulged in deficit spending with the economy already in high gear and unemployment low, the result was entirely predictable. Government spending, especially for the military, gives the economy a boost that creates jobs and puts money in many people's pockets. But such spending does not produce consumer goods: It merely increases consumer demand for privately produced goods that remain in short supply. So, flush with money, consumers are willing to pay higher and higher prices for whatever they can find. Result: inflation.

Adding to the inflationary pressure are all the businesses that seek loans to finance production and meet rising consumer demand. Those companies find interest rates going up and unemployment low, so they not only have to pay more to borrow, they also have to pay more for labor. Their current workers want higher wages to offset the suddenly rising cost of living, and the companies need to hire more workers to produce more goods and services. Unless they do all these things, they won't be able to compete.

Bingo! The inflationary spiral is off and running. Each new increase feeds the next, and before you know it, the overall economic situation begins to deteriorate. People on fixed incomes struggle just to afford the basics and thus fall farther behind in this bogus prosperity. Any interest income received from bonds stays the same, no matter what is happening to the prices they must pay for goods and services.

Furthermore, as interest rates rise, older bonds lose value because they pay less interest than new bonds. Accordingly, they can be sold only at ever more discounted prices. Rather than lose capital, lenders holding older bonds tend to wait them out, accepting the low interest in order to get the full price at maturity. The lenders' incomes fall. Striving to recover, they demand even higher rates of interest to make the next loan.

All this distorts values. At the end of the day, inflation gives rise to a string of broken promises—and trust, the glue of every society, comes undone.

Once such a spiral gains speed, it's never easy to stop. Nixon tried hard. True, his main assault on inflation was the ill-considered adoption of price controls, a remedy that few of his advisers expected to succeed. But to his credit, Nixon did manage to curb the growth of spending. He immediately reduced the share of the budget allotted to the war in Vietnam, and he cut the rate of growth of entitlement programs by establishing spending caps. Nevertheless, the Nixon budgets ran a deficit every year but 1969, when a 10 percent income surtax, passed at the end of Johnson's term (to help pay for the Vietnam War), produced a surplus. The red ink over the six years of the Nixon presidency totaled $67 billion.

Though the deficits were trending down in his last two years, Nixon, like Johnson, did something that had lasting and devastating budget consequences: In 1972, he approved a bill that permanently indexed Social Security benefits to the rate of inflation, thus stripping Congress of the power to withhold increases until fiscal conditions warrant, and virtually guaranteeing annual increases in the program's spending.

GERALD FORD

Whatever his talents and faults, Gerald R. Ford was the victim of a terrible run of bad luck. To begin with, he assumed the presidency under what he himself called "extraordinary circumstances"—not only did the national psyche need healing in the aftermath of the

DEFICITS UNDER FORD

1975   1976

100
50
0
-50
-100

-53.2

-73.7

TOTAL DEFICIT 2 YEARS: $126.9 BILLION

Watergate scandal and the Nixon resignation, but countries around the world needed to see that American democracy would prevail. The most visible representative of the United States and its democratic processes faced a daunting list of problems: inflation, economic lethargy, energy shortages, and a world fraught with danger.

When Ford replaced the resigning Nixon in 1974, his first problem was the recession that had begun the previous year. Following the lead of Roosevelt and Kennedy, Ford decided to use federal spending to restart the country's economic engines. In essence, he opted to pump up the deficit in order to create money for consumers to spend and thus revive demand and stimulate new production.

This tactic proved to be a mistake. Spending was already ratcheting up, because those citizens most affected by the recession automatically qualified for the entitlement programs Lyndon Johnson had initiated. Now Ford opened the deficit-making spigot even wider, first by getting Congress to pass a partial tax rebate for 1974 and then by pushing through a tax cut the following year. Whether or not these measures proved a tonic for the recovery, they worked like catnip on inflation, which spiraled higher with abandon. Ford's response was cautious, perhaps because of the criticism heaped on Nixon's price controls, and even less effective. He unveiled his "Whip Inflation Now" campaign, handing out WIN buttons to citizens and spotlighting a quartet of leading economic officials who brandished baseball bats as a token of determination. Although surely well-intentioned, Ford's jawboning was no match for the economic forces working against his policies.

JIMMY CARTER

One might almost pity one-term President Jimmy Carter, heir to the mistakes of three predecessors in a row. Johnson had begun the march of fiscal follies. Nixon, uneasy, had tried to curb military spending and the growth of entitlement programs, but his attempts to restore reason were no match for the rising tide of deficit financing. And then came Ford's series of tax cuts at a time of ballooning deficits. All this left Carter with a leadership choice between fighting or fleeing, greatness or mediocrity.

Unfortunately, Carter lacked the political will to cut back entitlement programs and to order big cuts in defense spending, the latter not really surprising in what was still the Cold War era. Nevertheless, his failure to act allowed a challenger, Ronald Reagan, to ask voters his famously lethal question: "Are you better off now than you were four years ago?" The electorate's resounding "No" surely hastened the end of the Carter presidency.

Carter's recession problems were, unhappily, magnified by a change in the economy. Not only had the peak wave of baby boomers entered the workforce, but growing numbers of women were now competing with men for jobs. Between 1973 and 1980, the number of working women jumped from 30 million to 40 million, a 33 percent increase in only seven years. So even though the economy resumed expansion, the growth was too slow to provide the number of jobs

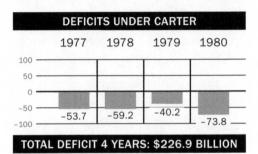

DEFICITS UNDER CARTER

1977	1978	1979	1980
−53.7	−59.2	−40.2	−73.8

TOTAL DEFICIT 4 YEARS: $226.9 BILLION

required. Carter chose to spur the expansion with—what else?—deficit spending. Result: "stagflation," the triple whammy combining slow growth, relatively high unemployment, and fast-rising consumer prices. In 1980, soaring interest rates pushed the prime rate—the rate commercial banks charge their top corporate borrowers—to an almost unthinkable 21 percent.

Even so, inflation might have produced a beneficial side effect by at least shrinking the percentage of the federal budget allotted to entitlement programs. Here's what I mean: If inflation runs at 10 percent, a benefit of $500 this year will be worth just $450 in next year's money, while tax revenues will rise even if rates levied on rising incomes hold steady. In just a few years, the entitlements burden will be considerably lighter because it is eating up less of the overall revenues.

But it wasn't to be: Congress intervened, arguing that it was unfair to penalize entitlement beneficiaries for inflation caused by government policies. In addition to the already-indexed Social Security benefits, lawmakers voted to link benefits for several major programs to the annual rise in the cost of living. In other words, from that day on, entitlement payments would rise relentlessly in order to make beneficiaries whole no matter how high inflation went. It was a boon for the people getting paid, but a road to doom for U.S. fiscal policy. Even if our leaders wanted to reduce spending—and they didn't— they were making it impossible. Reason: The rising number of people receiving indexed entitlements, plus the growing burden of interest payments (a certainty unless we want to default on our bonds) as the debt increased, meant that mandatory spending would climb as a percentage of the overall budget. With each year, less and less of the budget would be available for cutting.

The Carter years ushered in new records in annual budget deficits and growth of the national debt. During Jimmy Carter's term in the White House, the cumulative excess of spending over revenues came to nearly $227 billion, or more than all the deficits piled up during World War II. At the end of his term, the national debt totaled $930 billion.

One saving economic grace in Carter's Administration was his appointment of Paul Volcker to head the Federal Reserve. Volcker, as we shall see, is praised to this day for his well-fought battle against inflation.

RONALD REAGAN

When Ronald Reagan was running for president, we thought we knew one thing for certain: He was a fiscal conservative. But over his eight years in office, Reagan ran a deficit of $1.34 trillion, while the national debt nearly tripled to what was then a staggering $2.6 trillion. And whereas the United States had been the world's biggest creditor nation just 10 years earlier, it became the world's biggest debtor. Whatever his other achievements, Reagan failed at eliminating the deficit, curbing entitlements, and slowing the growth of federal spending.

Like Lyndon Johnson's, President Reagan's core mistake was his attempt to achieve two huge goals at once. He set out to gear up for an arms race so costly that any attempt to keep pace would bankrupt the Soviet Union. At the same time, he wanted to balance the federal budget. But Reagan was determined not to seek additional tax revenues to achieve either goal. Instead, he expected to get part of the

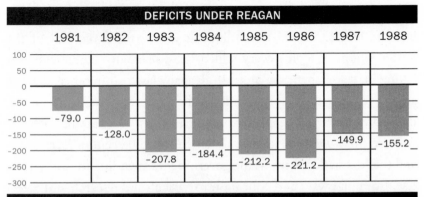

money by ending the government "waste, fraud, and abuse" he had been criticizing for years.

As for the rest of the missing funds, well, that would come from what his rival and eventual vice president, George H. W. Bush, memorably labeled "voodoo economics." Reagan planned to raise revenues not with tax increases but with tax cuts. These so-called supply-side cuts in tax rates would, in theory, persuade people to work harder and save or invest what they would have paid in taxes, thus fueling so much economic growth that total tax revenues would actually rise despite the cut in rates and without any severe offsetting spending cuts. If it sounds too good to be true, that's because it is.

Reagan pushed through two such tax cuts, in 1981 and again in 1986, and total tax revenues did rise—though far from quickly and in amounts nowhere near what was needed to mop up the red ink. And the crusade to reap savings from the elimination of waste, fraud, and abuse ultimately failed, because neither Congress nor the White House could break its addiction to spending. In any case, the plain truth is that there's nothing like enough waste, fraud, and abuse in federal spending to soak up deficits as big as Reagan was running. His last budget included a deficit of $155 billion, or more than half the total outlay that Congress could control.

With or without revenues to pay for it, the arms race went off as scheduled. Between 1980 and 1988, defense spending soared by 116 percent, going from $134 billion to $290 billion annually. Arguably, it had the desired effect: The following year marked the end of the Soviet Union. But, for every added tax dollar our government was taking in, it was spending $1.21. In Reagan's last year in office, defense ate up 32 percent of all spending, while 54 percent went for entitlement programs and 24 percent for interest on the national debt. If you add up those three items, they come to 110 percent of revenues— and that doesn't even count the government's spending for everything else, from highways and education to agricultural research and veterans' affairs. You can see the red ink spilling across your calculations.

We were beginning to run all nondefense programs on borrowed money, a pattern that continues today.

When all is said and done, Ronald Reagan was indeed the "Teflon President" his detractors wryly labeled him. On the one hand, he was widely billed as a steadfast slasher of personal and corporate income taxes. On the other hand, taxes were, in fact, increased by a very sizable amount on his watch. Taxes rose in every year of the Reagan presidency but one, 1988. Reagan's tax boost in 1982 came to nearly 1 percent of GDP, the biggest peacetime tax increase in history, and was followed by more new taxes in 1984, 1985, 1986, and 1987. The net effect, writes Bruce Bartlett in the conservative *National Review Online,* was a tax rise of some $164 billion under the Great Communicator. Most of the increases were slyly labeled not as taxes but as "revenue enhancements." In addition, Reagan approved Social Security and Medicare payroll-tax increases that to this day take ever-bigger bites out of taxable wages, as well as a gasoline tax increase. Even so, Reagan managed to run up massive deficits. But he was a leader so immune to bad news and held in such affection by his acolytes that he was given a pass for proclaiming that morning had come to America.

One unequivocal triumph did occur during the Reagan years: Paul Volcker, still chairman of the Federal Reserve System, engineered a long, painful squeeze on the money supply. By tightening credit, slowing job growth, forcing price cuts, and curbing wage gains, Volcker's policies eventually broke the back of inflation.

GEORGE H. W. BUSH

The first President Bush, like Democrats and Republicans before him, came to office facing formidable challenges—not least the effects of the enormous deficits and debt run up by his predecessor. The problems had been sown and nurtured through various administrations, of course, but the crisis point for Republican George H. W.

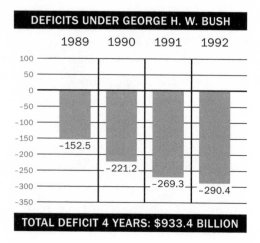

DEFICITS UNDER GEORGE H. W. BUSH

| 1989 | 1990 | 1991 | 1992 |

-152.5
-221.2
-269.3
-290.4

TOTAL DEFICIT 4 YEARS: $933.4 BILLION

Bush was so close at hand that he had few real choices. Thanks to the growth of entitlement programs and interest on the national debt, the controllable part of the budget had shrunk to a mere 33 percent. With the mountain of debt looking increasingly unstable, President Bush decided his only wiggle room was on the revenue side. Convinced that Reagan's supply-side tax cut was, indeed, voodoo economics, he agreed to a tax increase and fended off disaster.

Having campaigned on a pledge of no new taxes—cemented in the public's mind by his firm line "Read my lips"—Bush paid a heavy price in both political and personal popularity for his courageous attempt to get the budget under control. But, in the end, Bush, like the men before him, failed to wrestle the spending demon to the ground. In fact, aided and abetted by Congress, he supported environmental initiatives and the largest expansion ever in the Head Start preschool program. Mindful of the increasing deficit, however, he also proposed cuts in defense spending and in popular programs for the elderly and disabled.

Nonetheless, with a recession cutting tax receipts in the last half of his term, Bush senior managed to set still-larger records for spending in excess of revenues over the course of his four years in office. In those four years, he racked up a cumulative deficit of $933.4 billion— 70 percent of Ronald Reagan's total red ink in half the time. Day for day in office, Bush handily won the title of all-time champion spender—until his son came to Washington.

BILL CLINTON

An economic pragmatist, Democrat Bill Clinton needed little persuading from his advisers, notably Treasury Secretary Robert E. Rubin, to convince him of the dangers of the debt load and the huge and growing deficits he had inherited. To stop the hemorrhaging of budgetary red ink, Clinton, like the elder Bush, first chose to act on the revenue side: He persuaded Congress to pass what was arguably the single biggest tax increase in the nation's history.

Amplified by a long economic boom, the higher rates churned up a river of revenues—and for once, Congress did not move immediately to spend it all. Nor did Clinton press for increased spending without offsetting revenue gains. As a result, he cut the deficit every year he was in office, balanced the budget, and ended his run with solid budget surpluses. To his credit, Clinton also took a first step

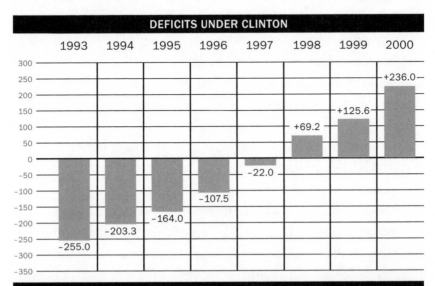

DEFICITS UNDER CLINTON

1993	1994	1995	1996	1997	1998	1999	2000
-255.0	-203.3	-164.0	-107.5	-22.0	+69.2	+125.6	+236.0

TOTAL DEFICIT 8 YEARS: $320.5 BILLION

down the road toward eliminating the national debt. During fiscal 2000, the federal government slashed its publicly held debt by $223 billion, the biggest single-year pay-down of debt in U.S. history.

When Republicans gained control of Congress in 1994, they moved to fulfill their campaign pledge to reduce wasteful government spending and eliminate the deficit. President Clinton confounded his critics and angered many of his supporters when he opted to go along with part of the Republicans' plan to balance the federal budget through cuts in welfare, food stamps, and other entitlement programs. Accused of abandoning core constituencies and punishing the poor, Clinton, like the elder Bush before him, risked political suicide in the name of fiscal discipline. After Clinton's first three years in office, nondefense discretionary spending had fallen by 0.7 percent. Testifying to the power of even a modicum of bipartisan cooperation were the sharply declining budget deficits of the Clinton Administration, which started in 1993 at $255 billion and plunged to $22 billion by 1997. In Clinton's last three years, he actually achieved budget surpluses.

How best to use those surpluses stirred considerable debate. It was perhaps inevitable, though, that when it came to actual choices, the surpluses would be spent rather than invested in the nation's future. Forty years of living beyond our means, without the wake-up call of another Great Depression to shake our confidence, had apparently convinced all but a few of our elected representatives that the consequences of fiscal recklessness weren't worth worrying about.

GEORGE W. BUSH

So perhaps it was not really surprising that, in the Administration of the second President Bush, steady growth in total spending became the order of the day, along with huge tax cuts that showered major benefits on the wealthiest Americans. If Clinton confounded his critics, George W. Bush has confounded critics and supporters alike.

Elected as a fiscal conservative, the President has paid little more than lip service to controlling government spending and, instead, has brought about huge increases in our national debt.

To be fair, Bush had a lot to cope with: the bursting of the stock market bubble and the ensuing recession; the terrorist attacks of September 11, 2001; corporate scandals; and the wars in Afghanistan and Iraq, all of which provided unexpected shocks to the economy. Bush ramped up spending and pushed through two consecutive tax cuts that were pitched as economic stimuli but, as it soon became clear, were aimed primarily at the wealthy, who would continue to enjoy the benefits long after the short-term recession. And on top of that came another huge increase in entitlement spending: Late in 2003, as U.S. efforts in Afghanistan and the occupation of Iraq continued to gobble up enormous sums of money while the threat from terrorism seemed to intensify rather than recede, a bipartisan congressional coalition passed a new prescription-drug entitlement for Medicare beneficiaries. It was estimated to cost $400 billion over the next

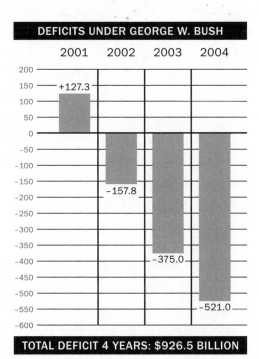

DEFICITS UNDER GEORGE W. BUSH

2001   2002   2003   2004

+127.3

−157.8

−375.0

−521.0

TOTAL DEFICIT 4 YEARS: $926.5 BILLION

decade—an absurdly lowball figure, as it turned out—and nary a mention was made about how the nation might pay for it. When it was later learned that the Administration had known all along the cost would be at least $534 billion and had pressured a program actuary to withhold the true cost from Congress and the public, the President's motives came under heavy fire. Like the spin used to push through Congress his enormous tax cuts in the face of record deficits, the Medicare cover-up fed fears that Bush's real motive may be the neo-conservative gambit called "starve the beast," a deliberate scheme to produce unsustainable deficits that will force a more limited form of government.

Even before the passage of the Medicare drug bill, the Congressional Budget Office (CBO) reckoned that the budget deficit for this fiscal year would be $500 billion, with cumulative deficits totaling some $2.9 trillion over the next decade. And the CBO's estimate for this year is less than the $521 billion deficit predicted by the Administration itself. This reversal of expectations is literally dizzying. As recently as May 2001, the CBO was forecasting surpluses totaling $5.6 trillion over 10 years. Somehow, $8.5 trillion has slipped through the administration's fingers in just three years. Where did it go?

Nor have we yet plumbed the depths of the red ink flooding over us in 2004. The CBO estimate doesn't include spending for military activities in Iraq beyond September 30, 2004, or items like the President's proposed tax credit for the uninsured to buy catastrophic health insurance—a break likely to soak up $65 billion in revenues in the coming years. And looking ahead, the Bush budget forecasts only five years out, ensuring that it will not factor in the full cost of making his tax cuts permanent, as the President advocates.

Democrats, of course, argue that the President's tax cuts are a major factor spurring the growth of the federal deficit, blaming them for as much as 60 percent of the increase. However, there's no doubt that the tax cuts stimulated the economy and generated at least some added tax revenues. The real problem is that the tax cuts were not matched by cuts in spending. As Pete Peterson, former commerce secretary in the Nixon Administration, wrote not long ago, "Long-term tax cuts without long-term spending cuts are not tax cuts. They are 'tax deferrals.'" That simply means the taxes will be paid by our children and grandchildren long after those responsible for the fiscal catastrophe have taken up residence elsewhere.

Indeed, far from being reduced, spending has risen. Part of it is the inevitable cost of defending against tyranny in the world. The Cato Institute, a conservative think tank, calculates that George W. Bush increased defense spending by about 34 percent in his first three years in office. But, the institute adds, nondefense discretionary spending jumped, too, by almost 28 percent. Congress and the President have backed the biggest education bill in history, the biggest farm bill in history, and the biggest expansion in any Great Society program (Medicare) since Lyndon Johnson introduced them.

Like leaders before him—from both major political parties—the second President Bush consistently fails to brake federal spending. In his 2003 State of the Union speech, he promised, "We will not deny, we will not ignore, we will not pass along our problems to other Congresses, to other presidents, and other generations." Yet he continues to propose ambitious new programs, including an expedition to Mars and a base on the moon, usually without adding price tags, as if money were someone else's problem. Moreover, he has never once (at least as of this writing) used his veto because a bill costs too much.

In his four years in office, Bush II will preside over a cumulative deficit of more than $926 billion. Given that he started with a year of inherited surpluses, his deficit-making capabilities surpass even his father's record-breaking clip. And so the younger Bush must accept his share of the blame for the nation's fiscal irresponsibility.

He wants to have it all—guns, butter, and tax cuts, too. Is that possible? No. As Al Broaddus, president of the Richmond, Virginia, Federal Reserve Bank, put it: "An increase in the production of defense-related goods and services must necessarily draw resources away from the production of other goods." In plain English, Broaddus said, "More guns means less butter at the national level."

The sad truth is that government has become so politicized as to make the idea of a common good little more than a nice, but unreachable, ideal. Both political parties and their members, those men and women whom you and I have elected to represent us in Washington, have been playing a cynical game for far too long. As the next graph shows, the predicament we now find ourselves in has been building for some time, but in the last three and a half years, the deterioration has been so great that we are on the edge of calamity.

If the deficits continue, and there's no reason to believe they won't with George W. Bush at the helm, we will soon find ourselves working and paying taxes largely just to finance the national debt. Indeed, based on Concord Coalition projections and my own calculations, a continuation of Bush's current spend-and-borrow policies will produce a total debt of more than $14 trillion by 2014. At last year's ultralow 4.6 percent interest rate—a rate that I can almost certainly guarantee will have risen since I penned these words—we would have to spend more than $644 billion just to pay the interest on the debt, or 28 percent of the $2.33 trillion of 2014 tax receipts projected by the Citizens for Tax Justice watchdog group. A rise in the interest rate to, say, 9 percent, a rate the Treasury paid on its 10-year bonds as recently as September 1990, would drive the interest cost on the debt to $1.26 trillion, or *more than half of projected tax receipts.*

The sad and scary truth is that George W. Bush's and Congress's tax cuts and runaway spending are eating away at our national strength. Contrary to their misleading assertions about the benefits the tax cuts provide to working families and their stimulative effects on the economy, even the Republican-controlled Joint Committee on Taxation has admitted that these cuts will most likely reduce long-term growth. That's because large deficits reduce savings and drain money away from the kind of productive investment that expands the economy. Huge debt and deficits can only lower our future living standards.

Time is growing short before our nation suffers the economic equivalent of September 11. I am not exaggerating the potential danger. But we can still turn things around and avoid disaster. To prevent it, all Americans—our political leaders and the voting population—have to act fast and decisively. The first step is for us to warn our elected leaders in simple terms: The jig is up. Your job is on the line. Face the facts, or quit politics.

Too dramatic? Too much trouble?

Ponder the graph—a vivid record of our ship of state as it crashes into colossal debt and begins sinking.

Remember: The passengers on this impending shipwreck include you and all your loved ones.

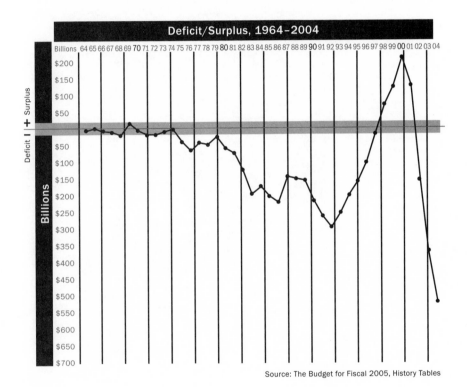

Source: The Budget for Fiscal 2005, History Tables

CHAPTER 4

LIES, DAMNED LIES, AND STATISTICS

WHEN IT COMES to spending the people's money, politicians of both parties long ago adopted a simple, cynical rule: Tell the people anything but the truth. Three-quarters of us are supposedly too bored, busy, or ignorant to care. And the rest of us? Well, you can hide nearly anything in a fog of big numbers.

The nineteenth-century British politician Benjamin Disraeli, once chancellor of the exchequer, was especially candid about the numbers caper. Mendacity, he said, takes three forms, in ascending order: "Lies, damned lies, and statistics."

And so it is with the U.S. federal budget deficit. The figure—$521 billion expected this fiscal year—is already horrendous. But it's a lie, only a fraction of the real horror story. Beyond it is a damned lie, and beyond that is a statistic. The progression reveals how all of us have been swindled by fast-talking politicians playing shell games that will hurt Americans for generations to come.

THE TREASURY'S WORTHLESS WONDERS

To get a whiff of how they've scammed the federal budget, imagine a sinking company that contrives an ingenious but totally illegal way out of its troubles. The chief executive floats a scheme to make the company's losses look much smaller—it won't end them, mind you, just hide some of them. But it's guaranteed to cushion the falling stock price and pump up the company's image.

His idea is brutally simple: Intercept the company's monthly contribution to the employees' pension fund and quietly use it to pay current expenses.

His management team listens silently. Nervous seconds pass. Suddenly, the biggest brownnose in the room hails the CEO as a hero; all his other courtiers leap in with obsequious variations on his inspired idea. It's a fawning frenzy. One vice president suggests calling the fund robbery a loan to the business, and a lawyer volunteers to draft the necessary papers. Another executive proposes an easy way to boost cash flow—just raise employee contributions to the pension fund.

Soon they're all high-fiving one another on how easy this rescue operation is going to be.

"Love it," all present agree.

The CEO duly calls a press conference aimed at legitimizing his blatant raid on the pension plan. He actually extols his team for helping employees in a time of trouble. With a moist eye, he declares, "Instead of decreasing our payments to the pension fund, my people had the guts to increase them!"

Reporters, detecting a fishy odor, question this self-serving spin. IRS gumshoes intervene, and the CEO and his coconspirators wind up being tried and convicted on numerous counts of fraud. For the next few years, they can ponder their sins while enjoying the hospitality of the Federal Bureau of Prisons. Good riddance.

The story is fictional, of course, but the crooked scheme it describes is essentially what's been done with a good chunk of your payroll taxes, the money you're obliged to pay toward your Social Security benefits. The schemers include four Presidents (Reagan, Clinton, and two Bushes), plus their congressional accomplices in both parties. They have steadily "borrowed" your retirement savings—$1.5 trillion at this writing—and used the money in ways that hide much of their runaway spending and mask the country's soaring deficits. Yes, they "repay" the Social Security trust fund, but not with real money. All we the people get in return are IOUs—special-issue Treasury bonds. Instead of paying interest you can save or spend, these worthless wonders pay interest only in the form of still more special bonds.

Even worse, these bonds have no market value because they can't be sold. Their only value is to the government, which can redeem the bonds by simply raising payroll taxes to pay off the bondholder—itself. In that sense, these special bonds aren't even IOUs. They're really "UOUs," quips Ed Henry, publisher of TUFF, the Taxpayers Union for Financial Freedom.

So it is pure farce when the government pretends to pay interest to the Social Security trust fund—at an average rate of around 4 percent in 2003, but often much higher, depending on market conditions. And it is downright fraud when government overseers claim they can pay part of the Social Security benefits owed to retirees out of the interest earned on the nonmarketable securities they themselves have issued. You could probably do better buying Baghdad Transit Authority bonds, if there were such a thing.

Here's the bottom line: While you steadily shovel money into the Social Security trust fund, year after year, the people you elect to represent your interests in Washington are just as steadily siphoning it out.

Shocked? You should be. You should also be mad as hell.

ALL POLITICS IS PORK

Where did the money go? Oh, just the usual. A highway to nowhere in the state of a senator whose vote some majority leader needed to pass one bill or another. Or, if Alaska Representative Don Young has his way, two bridges to nowhere. Young included his two pet projects in the national highway bill approved early in 2004 by the House committee he chairs (how convenient). One of the structures deemed worthy of financial support from taxpayers in the other 49 states connects Ketchikan, Alaska, to an island a mile away. Up until now, the 50 people who call the island home have managed just fine using the Ketchikan ferry. The other bridge would connect Anchorage with a small port that has only one regular tenant. If the projects survive the appropriations process, they will create hundreds of construction jobs—at a cost of $2.2 billion to taxpayers. As *The New York Times* observed in an editorial, "It might be cheaper just to pay everybody several years' salary."

Or how about the list of projects cited in this year's *The Pig Book,* published by the Citizens Against Government Waste. CAGW has documented $185 billion in appropriations pork since 1991. Even though our country faces a record $521 billion budget deficit this year and is fighting a war, Congress saw no reason to curb its institutional piggishness. Alaska Senator Ted Stevens, powerful Republican chairman of the Senate Appropriations Committee, didn't let down the folks back home: His state once again led the nation in congressional pork in 2003, according to CAGW, raking in $524 million, 26 times the national average and a whopping $808 per Alaska resident. (That's on top of Young's highway bill largesse, of course.) Hawaii came in second in the oinker sweepstakes, slurping up $494 million from the public trough ($393 per Hawaiian resident). By no coincidence, Hawaii's favorite son, Senator Daniel Inouye, serves on that same appropriations committee as the second-highest-ranking Democrat.

All told, Congress can take credit for lifting some $23 billion from taxpayers' wallets last year to finance a host of vital projects like these:

- $50 million for Iowa Senator Charles Grassley's pet pork project—a 4.5-acre indoor rain forest in his state that is supposed to increase "global understanding of how life works on Earth and how we can lead truly sustainable lifestyles in harmony with all of nature."
- $3 million for a program to encourage Florida kids to take up golf.
- $1.7 million for the International Fertilizer Development Center in Muscle Shoals, Alabama.

- $238,000 to the National Wild Turkey Federation in Edgefield, South Carolina.

With 10,656 pork projects tucked into 13 spending bills last year, the list runs on and on, slathering pork fat across the land—and helping to explain why the federal budget is showing record deficits. All these projects undoubtedly have some value; the question is, should federal taxpayers be picking up the cost? If Congress couldn't control its reckless spending, why didn't President Bush step in to veto any of these bills? Why, as America struggles with the growing burdens of defending our homeland against terrorism and waging war in Iraq, didn't he say no to a self-indulgent and greedy Congress? Isn't that what strong leadership is all about?

Bush's reluctance to stand up to Congress is a big reason why federal spending has skyrocketed on his watch. The Administration claims the higher spending is a necessary consequence of the war on terrorism. But it's hard to see how teaching kids in Florida to play golf and spending taxpayer dollars to promote wild-turkey hunting fits into that picture. But, then, a look at the turkey group's Web site suggests another motive. The turkey federation's CEO notes that the "more than 20 million hunters . . . are an economic and political force to be recognized." And recognized they were in grand, election-year fashion on April 8, 2004, when a busy President Bush himself led a group representing, among others, the turkey federation, the National Rifle Association, and duck, quail, pheasant, and ruffed grouse hunters on a three-hour tour of his Crawford, Texas, ranch. The CAGW flatly states that "in this time of war, too many elected officials are more interested in protecting their incumbency than in protecting the physical and financial security of the American people." It's plain to see who the real turkeys are if we taxpayers allow this kind of wasteful, self-serving behavior to continue.

Bad as these pet projects are, they seem modest compared with certain government contracts awarded to big companies, allegedly with the sotto-voce help of national politicians from a company's home state. Everyone's favorite suspect is the Halliburton Company, the big Houston-based oilfield services provider headed by Vice President Dick Cheney between his high-level jobs in the first and second Bush Administrations. Critics accuse Halliburton of using its influence with government insiders to win a series of lucrative no-bid contracts in Iraq worth more than $11 billion. Allegations of overcharges and kickbacks were still being investigated by the Pentagon at this writing, and Halliburton has denied any wrongdoing. Nonetheless, the Bush Administration's war on terror has proved enormously profitable for Halliburton, which has provided troop support (fuel, food, housing) in half a dozen countries and built prison camps in Guantanamo Bay, Cuba. It will also build an embassy in Afghanistan.

But when it comes to military-industrial pork, few companies can match the Boeing Company. Arizona Senator John McCain takes great pride in exposing the aircraft maker's heavily larded contracts, such as a $23 billion deal in which Boeing wants to lease up to 100 of its 767 airborne refueling tankers to the Air Force. Under fire as too expensive, unethical, and a particularly egregious example of political pork veiled in post-9/11 anxiety, the tanker deal was marked for cancellation by the Pentagon's inspector general, who called it a $4.4 billion rip-off. Charges that the aircraft specifications were "tailored to match the contractor's product and not the Air Force's needs" followed the disclosure that Darleen Druyun, the Air Force official who negotiated the contract, had discussed job possibilities with Boeing CFO Michael Sears before the contract was awarded. Druyun did indeed join Boeing after leaving the Air Force, and both she and Sears were later fired. In April 2004, Druyun pleaded guilty to one count of conspiracy, suggesting she will testify for the prosecution.

From the outset, critics said the unusual leasing arrangement would be more costly than outright purchase of the new tankers, which the Air Force described as a "critical" but unaffordable need. In hearings before McCain's Commerce Committee, the maverick senator said, "The Air Force appeared not so much to negotiate with Boeing as to advocate for it, to the point of appearing to allow the company too much control not only over pricing and the terms and conditions of the contract, but perhaps also the aircraft's capabilities." He cited an independent consulting firm's estimate that each $131 million plane should have been priced between $59 million and $95 million. The Pentagon's inspector general seemed to agree, concluding that the Air Force failed to do its homework before determining that Boeing's price was fair.

But while McCain jabs a sharp stick in Boeing's eye, the company can be sure its dozens of lobbyists will be using its $8 million lobbying budget to settle any queasy stomachs in Congress. And from all indications, the Air Force will need little prodding to kiss and make up with Boeing before structuring yet another sweetheart deal.

THE MYTHICAL LOCKBOX

Your retirement money hasn't gone just to pay for pork. You are financing the government across the board—farm subsidies, missiles, prisons, environmental projects, and, most recently, those tax cuts focused on the wealthy that have put us in the fast lane to bankruptcy.

The enormous Social Security scam traces back to the final years of the Lyndon Johnson Administration, when the numerous government trust funds were merged as a single entity in the overall budget (what later came to be called the "unified budget perspective"). But it wasn't until the Ronald Reagan era, when Social Security benefits began to significantly outrun payroll tax receipts earmarked to pay them, that the rip-off really started in earnest. Most people are still astonished to learn that the Social Security trust fund is not an enormous piggy bank in which contributions are carefully salted away until they are needed. Perhaps the surprise traces back to that "lockbox" farce played out during the 2000 presidential campaign. Remember George Bush and Al Gore both promising to put the Clinton Administration's budget surplus into a lockbox to protect Social Security? They wanted us to believe they were going to stash away actual cash money, when all they really intended to do was add more of those nonmarketable IOUs to a government ledger—nonexistent funds in a nonexistent lockbox. Instead, what we have in the Social Security program is basically a pay-as-you-go Ponzi scheme, with this year's contributions used to pay current retirees.

That system was bound to cause trouble, but it worked until a growing number of longer-lived retirees and a declining American birth rate caught up with us. In the early years of the system, 50 workers contributed to support every pensioner, so the payroll taxes needed to support the system were a relative pittance. By 1982, with more actual retirees on the books and living longer than the program's planners foresaw back in the 1930s, the trust fund was running dry.

So President Reagan named a special commission to "save Social Security" into the next century. It was headed by Alan Greenspan, now the Federal Reserve Board's iconic chairman but then a relatively obscure economist. It basically proposed an accelerated increase in payroll taxes, to 11.4 percent of wages split between employer and employee starting in 1984, and rising to 12.4 percent by 1990.

The ultimate tax increase was a combined 15 percent for workers and their bosses. The boost was even steeper for self-employed people: They had to pay the full amount from their own pockets (but could expense half the cost on their income taxes). The overall bite was made politically palatable by the argument that it amounted to forced savings for retirement. The new level of payroll taxes would generate big surpluses for years to come, and the surpluses would be invested to earn interest, growing large enough to help finance retirement for the enormous baby-boom population in the twenty-first century—or so President Reagan, Alan Greenspan, and the bipartisan panel promised.

The reality was radically different. In effect, the politicians turned the Social Security trust fund into an oxymoron: no fund and no way you could trust the government numbers.

By law, any surplus in the Social Security trust fund must be invested in Treasury bonds. That makes sense on one level: The piles of cash can't simply be stacked up in some gigantic storehouse. Investment in Treasury securities, however, means that the Social Security surpluses are being lent to the government, which deposits them in its general fund to pay the nation's bills. So the trust fund's "assets"— some $1.5 trillion's worth at year-end 2003—are really nothing more than IOUs from the government, which promises to pay them back, with interest, when the trust fund needs the money to pay retirees' benefits.

It's hard to see what else could have been done with the surpluses. The money might have been placed in relatively safe investments outside the government. Proposals on the table today would allow part of the funds to be put into private investment accounts, but some find that notion controversial because of the seemingly greater risk. (Mishandled, the money could easily disappear.) The surpluses also could have been earmarked solely to pay off the national debt—in effect, a form of national saving. But the debt in those days was still less than $1 trillion, and the huge surpluses would have retired it in short order, only to raise the issue again: What to do with the surplus cash? Given that dilemma and Congress's and the Administration's natural proclivities, it was hardly surprising that the politicians chose to take the money and spend it.

SPLURGING OFF THE BOOKS

As often happens, the real scam was in the accounting. The unified budget approach, which sees all government income and outlays as one lump, is generally considered an economically sound way of budgeting, and Social Security's operating surpluses and deficits have thus been included in overall budget totals since 1970. It began, innocently enough, as an attempt to get a better handle on exactly how much the government took in and paid out each year, and to give the financial markets a clearer sense of federal borrowing needs. It didn't take long, of course, for politicians to notice the inherent budget-finagling possibilities.

President Johnson used some of the extra cash to balance his final budget issued in 1969, thus giving Richard Nixon a surplus in his first year in office. But the amounts involved back then were small and didn't mean much one way or the other. It wasn't until 1983, when serious amounts of Social Security money started rolling in after the Reagan-Greenspan "fix," that the politicians realized just how useful this cookie jar full of surplus bucks could be for hiding growing deficits in day-to-day governmental operations.

Technically, Social Security is still "off budget," and its trust fund's books are kept scrupulously separate, with theoretical interest from the Treasury's IOUs mounting steadily. But the unified budget assumes that Social Security payroll taxes are part of the government's total revenues, making the trust fund's loans to the Treasury an accounting technicality. Result: The Treasury's borrowing turns magically into revenue, and the interest piling up on the trust fund's books doesn't count as spending.

That sleight of hand allowed the unified budget to show a federal deficit of $375 billion for 2003 and a projected deficit of $521 billion for 2004. But those figures are lies. If the Social Security trust fund were counted separately, it would have shown a surplus of $161 billion in 2003 and a projected surplus of $154 billion in 2004. The rest of the government would have shown deficits—the real excess of spending over revenues—of $536 billion in 2003 and a projected $675 billion in 2004. We've come a long way from the lie that the deficit this year will be $521 billion. So will it be $675 billion? That's the damned lie. The statistic is still to come.

Like the fictional corporate scam at the beginning of this chapter, this is pretty clever work by the politicians. And, as you can see from the graph on page 69, it has systematically distorted the official budget numbers, softening reported deficits and, in two cases, turning those deficits into apparent surpluses.

Of course, the confusion in the numbers is purely intentional. Congress categorizes things to suit its own purposes. An expenditure of $175.1 million to fill the Strategic Petroleum Reserve, for instance, is declared off budget to make total spending look smaller. Ditto the

$87 billion supplemental appropriation passed in 2003 to pay for continued military operations and rebuilding in Afghanistan and Iraq. While fighting over every dollar of discretionary spending, the President and Congress simply pretended that the $87 billion didn't count toward the discretionary ceiling, even though every other dime spent by the Pentagon was included. Two items, Social Security and the postal service, are required by law to be treated as off budget, while numerous other programs have been moved on and off over the years.

This year, off-budget outlays will total $381.5 billion—all of it designed to skirt budgetary controls while still proclaiming allegiance to fiscal discipline. Congress can set budget caps, as required by law, and then spend beyond them simply by declaring that some of the spending doesn't count. "It's hard for Congress to break the law because they make the law," explains Bob Bixby, executive director of the bipartisan Concord Coalition, a private economic watchdog group.

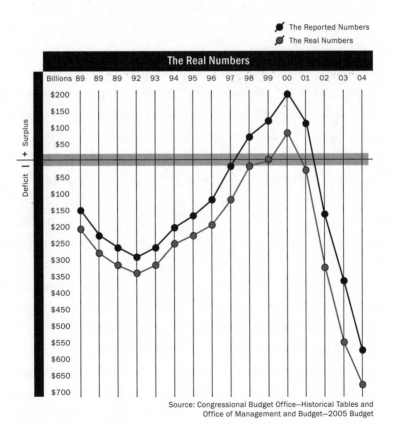

Source: Congressional Budget Office—Historical Tables and
Office of Management and Budget—2005 Budget

Not yet finished with their Social Security con job, the politicians decreed that the Treasury bonds and notes that went into the trust fund must be special, nontransferable securities, guaranteeing that the fund could never try to sell them—and also making sure that, if the government ever reneges on its promise to repay the loans, the fund will have nothing but worthless paper in its vaults. Then, rubbing salt into the cut, they decided that the Treasury would pay interest on its loans in the form of more of the same special securities—more worthless paper. With that stroke, the hijacking was complete.

SERIAL TAX KILLERS

What's more, there's growing evidence that something even more sinister has been going on in the hallowed halls of Congress. Democratic policy pundits claim that a dedicated group of radical legislators is intentionally spending us into insolvency to force the gutting of Social Security, Medicare, Medicaid, and virtually every other social program going back to the New Deal and the Great Society.

I don't believe in conspiracies as a rule, but a sober look at the effects of the last three-plus years of unfettered spending, coupled with enormous tax cuts mainly going to the wealthy, makes it hard to conclude that the deficits are just an unfortunate coincidence. A group of radical conservatives in our country openly advocates a policy known as "starving the beast." As noted earlier in this book, it holds that taxes—federal, state, and local—should be cut solely to compel drastic cutbacks in public spending. Grover Norquist, president of Americans for Tax Reform, is the most visible and vocal proponent of a group that wants to deprive the government of tax revenues and thus give it no choice but to downsize, to do away with the social programs that we have increasingly depended on since the Great Depression. By aiming the tax cuts primarily at the wealthy, and, if possible, raising taxes on the working class (dubbed "lucky duckies" in a *Wall Street Journal* editorial, because they pay lower taxes and benefit from entitlement programs), they hope that a majority of voters will come to hate the government, or so the theory goes. Boiling "with tax rage," they will turn on the government and rebel against paying any taxes at all.

The phrase "starve the beast" was first coined by Ronald Reagan's budget director, David Stockman. It has become the mantra for a 25-year crusade to cut taxes. It is preached by such spokesmen as Norquist, who once said: "I don't want to abolish government. I simply want to reduce it to the size where I can drag it into the bathroom and drown it in the bathtub." In another interview, he made it even clearer: "The goal is reducing the size and scope of government by draining its lifeblood." These radical conservatives preach fiscal discipline, but they go along with totally reckless spending combined with tax cuts, knowing that the crippling deficits inevitably will cause a train wreck fatal to the hated social programs.

By both word and deed, President George W. Bush has implied that he subscribes to this doctrine. In August 2001, as the Clinton surpluses were evaporating, he applauded the loss as "incredibly positive news," saying that now Congress would be placed in a "fiscal straitjacket." That same year, the Republican-controlled Congress under Majority Leader Trent Lott abolished the pay-as-you-go budget controls enacted by the first President Bush in 1990 and extended by President Clinton in 1993. Negotiated in a bipartisan effort, the caps had created surpluses by forcing Congress to offset new spending with taxes, or with cuts in other spending. A strong president leading a bipartisan effort and sounding the public alarm might have forced Congress to accept some fiscal discipline. Instead, Bush persuaded Congress to pass one massive new tax cut after another, and little in the way of bipartisanship can be found in the White House or in Congress, where the majority party steamrolls its policies through Congress.

The drive for tax cuts continued even after the war in Iraq, the recession, and the bursting stock-market bubble had driven us into record deficit spending. War almost always requires tax increases to pay its enormous costs. But just as Lyndon Johnson tried to downplay the cost of Vietnam, the Bush Administration refuses to estimate the cost of its operations in Iraq in its 2004 budget. Instead, war spending will be covered in another supplemental appropriation later in the year. Nevertheless, some Republicans in Congress are advocating still more tax cuts. With an astonishing lack of fiscal realism, House Majority Leader Tom DeLay insists, "Nothing is more important in the face of a war than cutting taxes."

Whatever President Bush's and Congress's real motives, by depriving the government of the revenues needed to run the programs we take for granted, and thus creating monstrous deficits that will eventually force deep cutbacks or huge tax burdens for future generations, they are indeed "starving the beast"—or possibly our grandchildren.

One can debate whether there is a reasonable rationale for continuing to cut taxes. But Americans need to understand what the consequences will be. If, as polls have indicated, Social Security is truly important to U.S. voters, we should at least know why we are about to lose it.

And whatever President Bush's role, nothing lessens the blame that Congress must shoulder. It had as much right to pull off its smash-and-grab caper with Social Security as a bank teller who rifles his cash drawer and lights out for Mexico.

THE STATISTIC

But we are not yet done with plumbing the full depth of the government's duplicity. The $375 billion deficit announced for 2003 is a lie; the $536 billion deficit is a damned lie. The statistic, the reality, is a deficit of $906 billion.

That's right—$906 billion.

In other words, we are overspending just shy of one trillion dollars in a single year. That's what Washington would have been obliged to report had the government kept its books the way corporations do.

There are two ways to record income and expense items—accrual accounting and cash accounting. One keeps businesses relatively honest, the other allows deception. Here's a brief description of each:

- Accrual accounting requires that all items, both incoming and outgoing, be recognized as soon as they are earned or incurred, even when they haven't yet been actually received or paid in cash. Public companies use accrual accounting, and with good reason: It compels them to set aside reserves for upcoming obligations, thus saving them from cash crunches while helping to protect investors.
- Cash accounting, which is used by most governments and most individual taxpayers, lets you put off recording income for tax purposes until you receive the actual cash and defer chalking up spending until the check goes out. You may also define your current worth as a simple right-now matter of annual income compared to annual outgo. This allows you to forget about your long-term debts and pretend you're much wealthier than you really are.

Guess which accounting method the federal government uses? Cash-basis, of course. By using it the government needn't confront the stupendous future cost of the promises it makes to millions of citizens who are counting on their Social Security and Medicare benefits. If a business were to enter a contract without reserves to meet the expense, it would be called an "unfunded liability," and the managers would be in hot water. But Congress makes its own laws—and with its collective head stuck in the sand, Congress needn't strive to control costs. It does not have to deal with the calamity ordinary people will face when the bills come due, long after the current President and many members of Congress are out of office.

Cash accounting is a devilishly simple way to maintain the illusion of solvency. By comparing only its current income and current outgo, the Social Security Administration reported a 2003 surplus of roughly $161 billion, which the government then hijacked to shrink its real budget deficit of $536 billion into red ink of only $375 billion. Had the managers used accrual accounting, as public companies must, the Social Security surplus would have morphed into a loss of some $370 billion, and the unified budget deficit would have ballooned to $906 billion.

Where would this loss have come from? In essence, the Social Security system is committed to paying about $14 trillion in benefits to current retirees and people who are now working, plus dependents and disabled people. But it has assets of only $3.5 trillion, an amount that includes all the payroll taxes current workers will pay over the rest of their working lives, plus the so-called trust fund of Treasury bonds that can't be sold.

In other words, there is a horrendous shortfall between liabilities and assets; last year, it came to $10.5 trillion, creating an unfunded liability of $370 billion more than the year before as more future benefits were promised to new workers. Using accrual accounting, the system would have had to set aside reserves to match that additional $370 billion liability. It would have reported a deficit of that amount—not the $160 billion surplus it claimed. And adding in all these extra billions would have forced the government to report a 2003 deficit of $906 billion.

AND NOW THE TRUTH

That is the statistic—another lie, a level of mendacity beyond lies and damned lies. But if accrual accounting were the standard throughout government, $906 billion wouldn't begin to measure the real deficit being racked up.

We aren't including Medicare, for instance, which has just assumed future obligations fuzzily projected at $10 trillion in the form of new benefits for prescription drugs. We aren't including the layered missile defense system ("Star Wars") that President Bush is resurrecting, a program that the CBO has said could cost up to $238 billion by 2025. We aren't counting the future costs of all those other major expenditures, such as President Bush's planned mission to Mars—estimated at anywhere from $40 billion to $600 billion! The dubious IOUs now sitting in the Social Security trust fund are themselves unfunded liabilities, which the government will be obligated to repay when real money is needed to cover retiree benefits.

If we could measure all the unfunded liabilities and give each its annual reserve, how much would the real, true, actual federal deficit come to? I'm an economist, and I'm used to thinking big, but that's not a calculation I'm up to making. It makes the mind reel and the spirit quail.

Fortunately, the job has been done for me. In the summer of 2003, economists Jagadeesh Gokhale and Kent Smetters published an exhaustive study done in 2002 for then–Treasury Secretary Paul O'Neill—a study conspicuously absent from President Bush's 2004 federal budget. Gokhale and Smetters used accrual accounting to find the total present value of future Social Security and Medicare obligations facing the government. They reached the mind-boggling sum of $44.2 trillion,

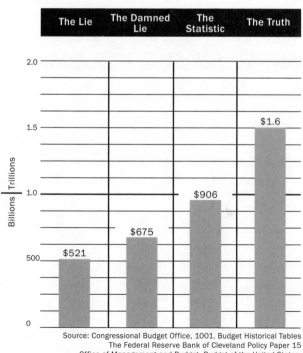

Source: Congressional Budget Office, 1001. Budget Historical Tables
The Federal Reserve Bank of Cleveland Policy Paper 15
Office of Management and Budget, Budget of the United States,
Fiscal year 2005
Congressional Budget Office—Current Budget Projections March 2004

reckoned at the end of fiscal 2002, or 10 times the government debt held by the public.

That unfunded liability will rise by $1.6 trillion every year we do nothing about it. That is the closest we'll come to discovering the genuine, gold-standard measure of our annual overspending. So the real deficit for 2004 is not the $521 billion lie, the $675 billion damned lie, or the $906 billion statistic. It's one trillion, six hundred billion dollars!

Gokhale and Smetters also laid out what has been called a menu of pain for solving the problem. We could cover the unfunded liability by raising taxes—a permanent increase of 16.6 percent in income taxes would have done it in 2003. Or we could end the problem by lowering the liability: Just make a permanent reduction of 45 percent in future Social Security and Medicare benefits. Another choice on the menu of pain: We could cut spending on other programs. But even if we cut all discretionary spending that Congress controls, including national defense, we still wouldn't cover the total unfunded liability.

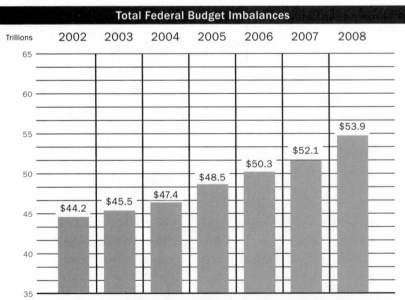

Total Federal Budget Imbalances

| Trillions | 2002 | 2003 | 2004 | 2005 | 2006 | 2007 | 2008 |

- 2002: $44.2
- 2003: $45.5
- 2004: $47.4
- 2005: $48.5
- 2006: $50.3
- 2007: $52.1
- 2008: $53.9

Source: Federal Reserve Bank of Cleveland, Fiscal and Generational Imbalances: *New Budget Measures for New Budget Priorities,* by Jagadeesh Gokhale and Kent Smetters, Policy Discussion Paper Number 5, p. 13, table 2

The best option seems to be some combination of higher taxes, lower spending, and reduced benefits. But every year we fail to act, the price will rise and the pain worsen. By the end of this year, the total future liability will be $47.4 trillion. At the end of 2008, the total will be $53.9 trillion.

Whatever degree of pain the menu choices inflict, we must brace ourselves and make them. Otherwise, the coming train wreck will strew economic fatalities across the landscape, dropping the United States to Third World economic status and setting off a worldwide depression.

And as the next chapter will show, this disaster could come far sooner than most people suspect. The trigger: a simple rise in interest rates.

CHAPTER 5

A CLEAR AND PRESENT DANGER

THE SOARING U.S. deficit is a potential catastrophe not only to the stability of our own economy and the economies of the entire world, but to your own personal solvency. This is not some abstract issue for newspaper editorial pages and talking heads on Sunday television shows. This crisis will affect every single American citizen. Everything you and your loved ones own is in clear and present danger, not to mention your very standard of living.

Why? Runaway deficits can easily propel interest rates so high that the home you toiled to own will suddenly become unaffordable. Those with adjustable mortgages will see their interest rates skyrocket and their monthly payments rise beyond their means. Worse, it will make it impossible for anyone to buy the house you now yearn to sell, driving prices down precipitously.

Remember this equation: higher deficits = higher interest rates and payments = increased inflation = financial collapse. Goodbye, house.

Let me show you how this disaster begins in the political funhouse of Congress, ricochets through Wall Street to your local bank, and winds up on your front lawn, destroying your dreams.

The U.S. government is a debtor, big time. And that's normal—all governments are debtors. But the Bush Administration, on the heels of the improvident practices of previous presidents, has thrown fiscal restraint to the wind, allowing its annual deficits and the national debt to rage totally out of control. We now have the biggest debt level in the history of the world—$7.3 trillion. Year after year, our government spends more than it makes, baldly denying that it is committing economic suicide. And President Bush and Congress, like crazy drivers with their feet mashed to the accelerator, have sharply increased the deficit each year.

One fragile fact has enabled Washington to handle its mushrooming debt, so far—the record-low interest rate it pays its lenders. But that illusory comfort is already ending. Interest rates are climbing—and when they climb high enough, our economy will begin to implode.

As interest rates rise, the government will have to slash essential services and programs, including, as you'll see in the chapters ahead, Social Security and Medicare. Higher interest rates will *burst* the housing bubble and bring the value of our homes crashing down. They will keep us from buying that new car we were eyeing (slamming the brakes on consumer spending) and send the cost of college loans into the stratosphere. They will drive the payments on our credit-card debt—now averaging $8,000 per household—and home-equity loans to unmanageable levels.

What can we do about this imminent crisis? First, let me walk you through the role debt and interest rates play in government and in our lives.

THE CREDIT MERRY-GO-ROUND

Debt is all about timeliness: You can spend years saving enough to pay cash for your dream house, or you can borrow the money and begin living your dream right now. The interest on your mortgage is the price you pay for your immediate satisfaction of owning a home (although, to help encourage home ownership, the government lightens the yoke with a tax deduction for those who itemize). It works the same way for the federal government. To spend what they want on programs they want to fund when the government doesn't have enough money to pay for them, the president and Congress allow the U.S. Treasury to borrow the needed cash by selling more and more of its bonds and bills. And just like the rest of us, the government has to pay interest on its loans.

Interest rates reflect, in part, the risks lenders assume when handing over their cash to borrowers. One risk, of course, is the possibility the borrower may simply not repay the loan. That is why low-income folks pay higher interest rates than the affluent. Another risk is inflation. Inflation decreases the value of the money lent over the course of the loan. Even if a lender gets back all the money lent, the purchasing power of the money will be less than it was at the time the loan was made. The longer the period covered by the loan, the greater the risk that inflation will eat away at the principal—and, consequently, interest rates will rise to compensate for the added risk.

In the credit market, as in all others, supply and demand rule, as interpreted by the Federal Reserve System and reflected in the regular auctions at which lenders bid for Treasury securities. These auctions are immense—the Treasury sold $3.7 trillion worth of bonds in 2002 alone—and they are ongoing.

Your checking account offers a simplified version of how supply and demand affect interest rates. The cash you put into a checking account is a loan to the bank, which uses your money to run its business and make loans to other people. You can withdraw cash from your checking account at any time, so your inflation risk is slim—and so is your interest-rate reward. A certificate of deposit carries a higher inflation risk, and a higher interest rate, because you have to hold it for a longer period of time or pay a penalty.

When the supply of credit in the nation as a whole rises, when lenders are eager to dole out their cash, borrowers can afford to be picky—and lenders charge lower interest rates to beat out the competition. By the same token, if credit is in short supply, it's the borrowers who must scramble to tap a restricted pool of cash, and the lenders will charge as much as a competitive market will bear. As a result, interest rates rise.

The Federal Reserve System actually sets only one interest rate, the overnight fee it charges banks on the short-term borrowings they make to cover their reserve requirements. But its indirect power is far greater. The Fed alone has the power to pull money out of the market or flood the market with new money—money created from nothing—and thus nudge interest rates up or down by adjusting the supply of money. If it wants rates to fall, it buys Treasury securities from the big banks, and the Fed's checks to pay for them become money in circulation, increasing the money supply and thus pushing the rates down. To nudge rates up, the Fed sells Treasuries and soaks up funds to reduce the supply of money in circulation.

The Fed's interest-rate operations are based on its perception of the overall state of the economy. Its goal is to keep the economy growing at a healthy rate with stable prices and high employment. But all sorts of other things can influence the supply of credit in the economy. The last time you postponed paying your credit-card bill, for example, you effectively reduced the cash available to the sponsoring bank and, therefore, the amount of cash it could lend to its customers. If enough Americans followed your lead, it would spark a short-term credit crunch and thus an increase in the nation's interest rates—unless, of course, the Fed moved alertly to counter the trend.

By and large, though, the Fed's power over interest rates dwindles as loan periods lengthen. When the Treasury offers its 10-year bonds, the only real factor is the willingness of lenders to buy them. If there aren't enough investors willing to buy at 4 percent, the Treasury has to offer 4.1 percent, and then perhaps 4.2 or 4.5, and so on up to 15.84 percent, the highest rate on record, set in September of 1981. Despite rising rates, the Treasury can't withdraw its offering. Maturing bonds have to be rolled over, and the new deficit has to be financed. Otherwise, some government program would have to be halted because we couldn't afford it—and who ever heard of an embarrassment like that?

ON THE BRINK OF RUIN

Our fiscal crisis today arises from our government's sheer extravagance—spending so crazy that this year's federal deficit will hit a record $521 billion. And again, that isn't even the real number: If you include Social Security borrowing, various accounting tricks, and the cost of war in Iraq, the deficit is much larger—nearly *$1 trillion.* Not surprisingly, President Bush and his cronies prefer the lower figure.

What does a revenue shortfall of $521 billion mean? It's more than all our cities spend in an entire year on police, fire protection, medical care, and every other service they provide, combined. It's more than we would save annually by abolishing both Medicare and Medicaid in their entirety. It works out to $1.4 billion a day, or more than $40 billion a month.

Think about it: Every day, our government is spending $1.4 billion more than it takes in. In October 2003, the first month of fiscal 2004, U.S. spending exceeded revenues by an all-time monthly high of $69.58 billion. That's right, we were short nearly $70 billion in a *single month.* Three decades ago, a full-year deficit of $69-plus billion would have been considered alarming. Now it is just one more barrier President Bush and our Congress have shamelessly hurtled through, with no apparent thought of the consequences.

To finance this horrendous level of deficits and debt, America is paying a heavy price—huge interest payments to all the domestic and overseas lenders that have bought our Treasury bonds. Our interest payments of $318 billion in 2003 were the government's third-biggest expense (after Social Security and the military). They consumed 24 percent of its income tax revenues. In other words, even at the historically low interest rate of 4.6 percent, debt payments siphoned off 24 cents of every dollar collected from income taxes in 2003. Imagine that you, like our government, were spending 24 percent of your income just to meet the interest charges on your credit-card bills. Now imagine what would happen if your credit-card company suddenly doubled the rate of interest it charges you. Could you meet your financial responsibilities? Not without cutting back on other expenditures: gym memberships, new clothes, food, housing, or your children's education. Perhaps all of them.

But as bad as the interest-payment figures are now, they are about to get worse. As the Treasury's bonds and notes mature each year, we have to borrow more and more just to keep our heads above water. Even if our national debt suddenly stopped growing and stood stock-still, rising interest rates would put us in grave danger. Trouble is, the debt just keeps getting bigger and bigger. Using Concord Coalition projections and then adjusting for the hidden deficit borrowing from the trust funds, I calculate that the national debt will rise to $8.077 trillion in 2005, jump to $8.693 trillion the year after that, pass the $9 trillion mark in 2007, and so on. By 2013, we will be staring down the barrel of a $14.045 trillion national debt.

Since George W. Bush took office, he and the current Congress have turned the United States into the world's leading spendthrift. Each annual deficit has been sharply higher than the year before, continually adding to the total debt and dangerously increasing the amount of interest we must pay. Hour by hour, day by day, our leaders are digging us into a deeper and deeper hole.

Yet all that is but a drop in the proverbial bucket compared to the toll that sharply rising interest rates will take on each and every one of us.

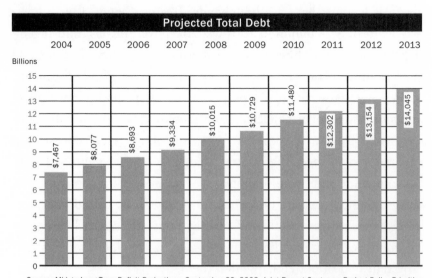

Source: Mid- to Long-Term Deficit Projections, September 29, 2003, Joint Report Center on Budget Policy Priorities of the Committee for Economic Development, the Concord Coalition, and author's calculations

A MOUNTAIN OF DEBT

For years now, we've lived in a fool's paradise. In 2000, after the stock-market bubble burst, America's economy began to slide toward recession. The Federal Reserve responded with a series of interest-rate cuts. By making borrowing cheaper, the move stimulated the economy and went a long way toward preventing a worse recession. But it also had a sharply negative effect. It encouraged newly elected President George W. Bush and our leaders in Congress to indulge in their deficit spending binge, since the interest on their borrowings would be minimal (relatively speaking, that is).

These annual deficits quickly built a mountain of debt on top of the existing $5.7 trillion. Yet President Bush and Congress seemed blind to the fact that interest rates would eventually start to climb. Now the climb has started.

Why are rates rising? One reason is inflation. It shrinks the value of a dollar, so you end up paying more for everything. A shrinking dollar is a good thing if you owe a lot of money at a fixed rate; it means you're paying off your debt with dollars that are worth less than the dollars you borrowed. But it's bad news for most people, including those whose loans carry a variable interest rate, not to mention retirees and others who live on fixed incomes. They can only watch helplessly as their purchasing power is whittled away. If the rate of inflation in the United States exceeds that of other nations, our products become less competitive overseas. Finally, inflation undermines our national confidence. It makes both companies and individuals nervous about the size of the inevitable price increases coming just around the bend, so they spend less. (Indeed, sharply rising gasoline prices in the spring of 2004 were credited with a drop in retail spending by low- and middle-income shoppers.) And spending cutbacks can increase unemployment and slow the economy enough to create a recession.

The Federal Reserve is dedicated to maintaining a healthy level of economic growth. When inflation rises much above 3 percent, it's a sign that the economy may be overheating, and the Fed intervenes by raising interest rates. The worse the inflation, the higher the interest rates go.

In the spring of 2004, consumer prices in the United States rose at an annualized rate of 5.1 percent. Oil and gasoline prices were soaring, but so were such disparate price tags as Disneyland admissions (up 6 percent) and paper towels (up 6 percent or more). The cost of steel was up 75 percent over the previous year, while the price of commodities like corn and soybeans jumped, too.

The signals that the Fed would have to increase interest rates were growing more pronounced.

Inflation has another way of nudging interest rates up. Lenders, already unhappy about the existing low interest rates, find themselves being paid off in depreciated dollars. That further stokes the pressure to raise interest rates. For holders of Treasury bonds, in the United States and abroad, inflation gives them more reason to stop buying Treasuries, and that in turn shrinks the credit market. Now the Treasury is forced to compete with other would-be borrowers for a smaller pool of credit. Higher interest rates may be the only way to lure investors back into the market.

The very weight of our more than $7 trillion debt will eventually produce just such a scenario. At some point, this unstoppable force of inflation will overwhelm the market and the Federal Reserve's attempts to control it.

What do I mean? The government's marketable debt already accounts for 25 percent of the entire U.S. credit market, and that number is bound to increase. As deficits soar, the government will be forced to borrow more and more, battling other borrowers for the limited funds. This competition will inevitably bid up interest rates on Treasury bonds and bills. When rates begin to rise against a backdrop of reckless budgetary policies and unsustainable trade deficits (I'll discuss the looming disaster of our trade deficit in the next chapter), lenders assume more inflation is on the way and then demand even higher rates to protect themselves.

Worse, the Treasury may not be able to sell all its bonds in the open markets if buyers decide the risks of buying them are too great. If that were to happen, the Federal Reserve would have to step in to buy the unsalable bonds, in effect printing new money to do it. This new money would push prices and rates ever higher, sending inflation soaring and leaving lenders holding the bag.

Any way you slice it, the risks posed by this massive overhang of debt are enormous and, ultimately, fatal to our economy.

Rising interest will eat up more of the tax revenues needed to keep the government going. Let me show you what happens to our government's projected 2004 income tax revenues of $1.3 trillion as the rates climb.

At a 6 percent interest rate, our interest payments climb from the current $318 billion to $419 billion—32 percent of our income tax revenues. At 10 percent, we need $697 billion just to pay the interest—approaching 54 percent of tax receipts. At 12 percent, interest rises to $837 billion—64 percent of our available tax dollars.

And if I factor in the kind of inflationary pressures that hit the United States in the early 1980s? In those days, interest rates—spurred by an oil crisis (sound familiar?)—of 18 percent were common. Applied to our 2004 debt, that rate would force us to pay our lenders $1.256 trillion in interest—more than 96 percent of our projected income tax revenues. The $44 billion pittance left in the federal till would barely cover the administrative expenses for Social Security, let alone monthly checks to retirees. And every other function of the federal government, including defense, homeland security, education, and Medicare, would have to shut down or be funded in some other way.

ROADKILL FROM A JUMP IN INTEREST RATES

If rising interest rates gobble up a major chunk of the government's income, our leaders would be forced to reduce or eliminate services and programs. As I pointed out earlier, entitlement programs like

Social Security and Medicare *would likely be the prime targets*—there is precious little cutting room elsewhere.

I discuss how such reductions in service might be accomplished in Chapter 7, but this much is clear: Such Draconian cuts would be painful for many Americans, particularly retirees. Smaller payments might force later retirement, or push many retirees back into the workforce. Lower medical benefits might lead to postponed treatment or premature death.

A spike in interest rates would also rapidly deflate the value of homes across the nation, a major pillar of the economy. Many people would be left holding on to houses that are worth less than what they paid for them. That's right, if the market were to collapse, the value of your house could easily plunge below—well below in some cases—the unpaid balance on your mortgage. Homeowners might abandon properties that were under water, rather than continue to make their mortgage payments. How's that for puncturing the American Dream?

When interest rates began to plunge in 2001 (and continued in 2002 and 2003), millions of homeowners raced to refinance their mortgages; banks saw $2.2 trillion in refinancing in 2003 alone. The lower payments resulting from the "refis," coupled with homeowner draw-downs of large chunks of their home equity, left families with a bundle of cash, the spending of which has helped buoy the economy ever since.

America went on a house-buying spree. Between 1999 and 2004, mortgage borrowings jumped 50 percent, from $4.4 trillion to $6.8 trillion. The banking industry helped inflate the housing bubble by offering all sorts of exotic ways to purchase a house or trade up, including low or zero down payments, interest-only monthly payments with a "balloon payment" of the entire principal later on, even a first mortgage for more than a home's value. Fixed-rate mortgages gave way to adjustable-rate. You might pay almost $600 a month for each $100,000 borrowed on a 30-year fixed-rate mortgage, but the adjustable-rate version would cost about half that amount. Of course, when interest rates go up a mere two percentage points, that $333 is going to increase to the level of the fixed-rate numbers, which already may be far beyond a family's ability to pay, and the rate is still susceptible to further increases.

Rising interest rates will inevitably discourage potential first-time buyers, and fewer buyers will lower the value of every home on the market. So much for those who were counting on selling their home (or taking out an annuity against it) to supplement their retirement income. They will have to revise their plans.

The interest rate disaster described here is just waiting to happen. It is part and parcel of the reckless, shameful fiscal behavior of our leaders in Washington. It is a clear and present danger to the future of our nation.

A RISING CHORUS

I am outraged and terrified over these issues, and I am not alone. In the summer of 2003, three of the country's most respected economic watchdogs—the business-oriented Committee for Economic Development, the nonpartisan Center on Budget and Policy Priorities, and the bipartisan Concord Coalition—issued a joint statement calling recent policy "the most fiscally irresponsible in American history." They bluntly forecast that the national debt would rise by *$5 trillion* over the next 10 years, not including the money borrowed from the trust funds.

While that stirred major ripples in academic circles, it hardly made the nightly news. Baffling numbers and subtle explanations proved to be too much heavy lifting for most newscasters. That is why we can't expect them to shed much light on the perils ahead until we actually crash into them.

But the number of people sounding the alarm is growing, and their ranks include some heavy hitters. Earlier this year, for example, the International Monetary Fund issued an unusually direct warning of the "significant risks" that chronic U.S. deficits pose for the entire financial world.

Former Treasury Secretary Robert E. Rubin, architect of the short-lived budget surpluses of 1998 to 2001, said recently that the Bush Administration's political promises of shrinking deficits simply aren't credible. He warns of the danger of "fiscal and financial disarray" (i.e., panic), both in world markets and in the U.S. economy.

David Walker, who runs the General Accounting Office, has said flatly that "our projected budget deficits are not manageable without significant changes in the status quo programs, policies, processes, and operations." Walker can openly speak his mind because his government appointment runs for 15 years. Others don't enjoy such freedom.

Even Alan Greenspan, who, in general, has supported each Administration's policies, and Paul O'Neill, the first Treasury secretary under President Bush, have taken issue with the Administration's stubborn insistence that its huge deficits don't matter. They have told Congress that the deficits do matter because they push up interest rates and eventually depress the economy. Greenspan has called for cuts in Social Security and Medicare benefits, acknowledging that the cost of these entitlement programs will rise dramatically with the retirement of the baby boomers. Given the size of the debt and the cost of paying for it, there won't be near enough money to go around.

My point is that this prognosis is not an alarmist's doomsday scenario, but rather a sober, even understated, down-to-earth analysis of the likely results of our rapidly escalating national indebtedness. Until now, those of us who shared these concerns had trouble being heard above the din of well-placed congressional and presidential defenders of the status quo. If the country we love is to survive, we must change the dialogue—and quickly. We must all raise our voices to demand that Congress and the President mend their profligate ways.

In the next chapter, I explore the disturbing implications of our increasing dependence on foreign investors to keep our heavily mortgaged government afloat. Today, they hold nearly 40 percent of our Treasury obligations. Not only do we send $100 billion in interest payments abroad every year, we also risk putting control of our economy at the mercy of other countries.

CHAPTER 6

THE LOOMING TRAIN WRECK OF THE TRADE DEFICIT

THE PEOPLE OF Shunde like to think big. Shunde, located in Guangdong Province, is one of China's awesome new manufacturing centers that have sprung up like toadstools from empty farmland to pour a rising tide of goods into the world. It bills itself as the "worldwide kingdom of the microwave oven," and its production lines run nonstop. They churn out a river of inexpensive appliances and other manufactured goods that the city's managers happily ship overseas, mostly to avid U.S. consumers. Shunde's civic conviction is clear: Anything America can do, Shunde can do better. Last year, the city replaced its municipal building with a carbon copy of the U.S. Capitol—only bigger.

Most of China seems to have the same blend of envy and swagger toward America. "Extravagance has gone deep into the bone marrow of U.S. society," proclaims Su Jingxiang, a research fellow with the China Institute of Contemporary International Relations. Writing in the *People's Daily Online*, he claims that the United States has changed "from a productive society to a nonproductive society," one in which "consumption and luxury are the real objectives."

If that sounds somewhat contemptuous toward us, Su Jingxiang has facts to support it. The U.S. trade deficit with China alone (i.e., the excess of imports over exports) reached a record $124 billion in 2003, meaning we lugged home $124 billion more in Chinese-made goods and services than China bought from us. At the same time, our overall trade deficit with our global trading partners soared 10 percent last year alone, reaching an unprecedented $489 billion. That is more than we spent in 2003 on Social Security, and it's twice the bill for Medicare.

The United States, a country that used to dazzle the world with its manufacturing productivity and inventiveness, now depends on imports. With 5 percent of the world's population, we are soaking up 20 percent of the world's exports. Month after month, year after year, we buy clothing and cameras, television sets and DVD players, computers and cell phones, microwave ovens and minivans—an endless stream of foreign-made goods, whether we can afford them or not. And most critically, we buy oil. We are the world's largest importer of oil, a dependency that adds tens of billions of dollars annually ($133 billion in 2003) to our trade deficit. (We also maintain a dangerous and precarious control over worldwide oil trading—and world trade in general—because oil trading is conducted in dollars. The consequent threat, as I'll discuss momentarily, is a hair-raising one.)

As the comic-strip philosopher Pogo put it, we have met the enemy, and he is us. Examine the label on your clothes, the manufacturer's information on your furniture, your computer, your car. Chances are, most are made abroad. The guy who answers your computer help-line call probably lives in Bangalore, India. In all, only a third of what Americans buy these days is actually made in the United States. Wal-Mart, a company whose founder, Sam Walton, used to boast about buying American, imported $12 billion worth of goods from China alone in 2003, making it China's eighth-largest trading partner, bigger than Britain or Russia.

GOBBLING UP THE WORLD'S GOODS

The reason for our escalating trade deficit is quite simple: We are a nation of consumers rather than savers. Americans save and invest less than citizens of any other industrialized country. Depending on how savings are measured, our national savings rate, which has been declining since the early 1990s, is down to 1 percent to 2 percent of our income. The stock-market bubble only accelerated this trend, as Americans experienced a wealth effect from the buildup of their stock equity and, as a result, saved less and consumed more. Thanks to a strong dollar, imports were cheap compared to domestic goods and increasingly gained cachet.

Today we are encouraged by our financial institutions and America's corporations to go into hock to buy everything we think we need as well as anything and everything we want. We've become addicted to the low costs and high quality of foreign-made goods—for proof, look no further than the explosive growth of megastores like Wal-Mart. We now have a substantial trade deficit with nearly every country in the world. Canada, our largest trading partner, sold us a record $54 billion more than it bought from us last year; Mexico chalked up a $41 billion surplus, also a record. Our deficit with Japan actually shrank slightly, but only because Japan—like South Korea and Taiwan—has transferred many of its assembly operations to China, where low-wage workers put products together inexpensively and ship them to us. This, together with our own corporate offshore operations there, has boosted our deficit with China to the all-time record for any country.

Why is this a bad thing?

If a nation is to remain strong and healthy, it needs to maintain a long-term balance between what it sells and what it buys. It's not all that different from your own household budget: If you spend more than you earn, you're going to be forced into deficit financing—running up credit-card charges, arranging a loan from your bank, or begging a few bucks from your brother-in-law. America's "brother-in-law" turns out to be Canadian and Mexican and European and Chinese. We borrow the savings of citizens in those countries and others to fund our consumption and investment, because every last penny of the small sums we do save goes to cover the high-flying lifestyle of our own Uncle Sam.

So all-consuming is our addiction to buying that we are willing to go deep into debt, both individually and as a country, to satisfy it. And as the words "Made in the USA" take on the scratchy sound of a hand-cranked Victrola, a sea of red ink spreads across our side of the international trade ledger.

Before 1975, we ran consistent surpluses in the balance of trade. We were the world's largest creditor nation. Today, we have had 29 straight years of trade deficits and have long since become the world's champion debtor. Our total foreign debt, just $350 billion in 1980, is now over *$3.6 trillion,* nearly 30 percent of our gross domestic product. And the deficits are growing at a frightening pace. In just the past five years, we have added $1.9 trillion to our total foreign debt. That's about 10 percent more than the total tax revenues our government collects in a year.

For most of the twentieth century, the United States boasted a surplus in trade. We sold far more than we bought. As the cornucopia of the world, we poured forth dependable, high-performance products that improved the lives of people everywhere. Our economic engine was the envy of the world. In the 1990s, the United States was racing along at a 3.3 percent annual growth rate while Europe was

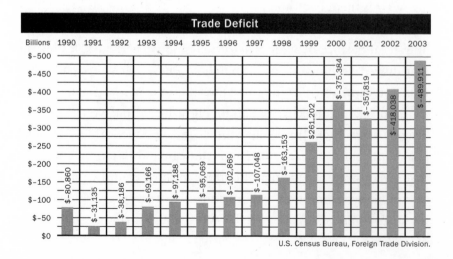

U.S. Census Bureau, Foreign Trade Division.

registering only 2 percent growth and Japan 1.3 percent. But, paradoxically, our strength and rapid growth ultimately helped to exacerbate the trade deficit because it nourished an appetite for cheap imported goods. At the same time, we were aiding and encouraging other nations to improve their own economic fortunes, in part so they could better afford to consume more of what we produced.

But the global spread of capitalism and the revival of once-moribund economies proved to be a two-edged sword. As other nations revved up their productive capacity, they not only began to match us in quality, they undercut us in price. And as the century wound down, so did America's industrial dominance: Our share of world manufacturing tumbled from 60 percent in 1950 to only 25 percent today. New, low-cost industrial powers took over much of the global market for manufactured goods, including the market here in the United States.

Americans complain, with at least some justification, that the playing field is tilted against us, with foreigners taking advantage and coming out ahead. We argue that:

- Foreigners block their markets with tariffs, quotas, and subsidies for domestic producers, while our economy is open to free trade.

There is some truth in this. The U.S. market is more open to imports than other economies, and the high nontariff barriers in foreign markets have been an important cause of the U.S. trade deficits. But we are far from innocent when it comes to trade barriers. In the past 18 months, the World Trade Organization has condemned U.S. restrictions on imports of steel and cotton. Our subsidies to domestic growers of rice, corn, and wheat effectively freeze Third World producers out of our markets. On balance, we're probably as much the sinner as we are sinned against.

- Our businesspeople just can't compete with low foreign costs and wages.

It's a challenge. But we can and do find plenty of buyers for our goods and services; in fact, the United States is the world's largest exporter in total dollar volume. The problem is that we buy even more.

• The dollar is overvalued. This makes our exports too expensive for foreigners, while imports can easily underprice goods made here.

For many years, the dollar was extremely strong, mostly because the United States was such an attractive country in which to invest. Investors could get higher rates of return in the United States than they could elsewhere. But in recent times, the dollar has been sinking fast against the euro, the British pound, and the Canadian dollar; it has lost about 30 percent of its value against the euro in the past two years alone. Meanwhile, countries like Japan and China are keeping the value of their currencies artificially low to foster export-driven growth policies. China, for instance, has pegged its yuan at a fixed rate to the dollar, refusing to let it fluctuate, and Japan is doing its best to keep the yen from rising. This has kept Asian goods underpriced in dollar terms. This part of the playing field is seriously biased against us, and U.S. officials have been pressuring both China and Japan for a more accommodating policy—so far, without success.

It stands to reason from an economic perspective that the falling dollar should encourage substantially more exports to Europe, while imports into the United States should be dropping as their dollar prices soar. But our trade deficit with Europe actually rose by 14 percent last year, partly because of Europe's sluggish economy, but also because of our unquenchable thirst for oil. And the recent surge in oil prices is only widening the deficit.

• It's the fault of globalization. Our multinational companies are moving production and jobs offshore to make bigger profits.

Undeniably true. Some say that's the name of the game: Capital will flow to wherever production is most efficient. But current U.S. trade and tax policies encourage and reward companies that move jobs overseas. In the past three years, 2.7 million manufacturing jobs have vanished from the United States, and the outsourcing of service jobs, such as computer programming and call-center work, has become a major political issue. Jobs that would pay as much as $100,000 in the United States are being performed abroad for a fraction of that amount. Many argue that there isn't much America can do to stop this tide or even slow it down. A serious look at our tax policies is in order. If we are providing tax incentives to move jobs offshore, we should eliminate them. If we choose not to eliminate the incentives, then we should level the playing field by providing firms with incentives to keep jobs at home. In that regard, the proposal by Democratic presidential challenger John Kerry to provide tax incentives to manufacturers who produce goods and expand their operations in the United States deserves consideration.

One theory that inspires virtual unanimity among economists is that two-way international trade is good for a country. It allows domestic businesses to move into new markets, boosting sales, employment, and economic growth. At the same time, it gives the public access to goods and services that may be better and/or cheaper than home-grown alternatives, thus raising standards of living. Increased international competition has also helped tame inflation in the United States by reducing the pricing power of U.S. companies. The glut of imports has acted as a safety valve to stem inflationary tendencies.

So whatever they say for political reasons, nearly all economists see globalized free trade as another step in the long improvement of living standards that began when newly efficient farm production sent a tide of displaced workers into town, where they found factory jobs and better lives. Today, many lost U.S. manufacturing jobs are being replaced by innovative and creative work in high technology, communications, and the entertainment industry. No one discounts the pain felt by individual workers who lose their jobs, but, on balance, our unemployment level has declined in the past decade—and our standard of living has risen. Furthermore, increased foreign capital inflows have permitted the U.S. economy to achieve higher rates of business investment. And if the money we borrow from foreigners goes to finance productive investment, the U.S. economy will benefit in the long run.

But there's a major caveat to all this: Our total debt to foreigners is rising to dangerously high levels.

DOLLARS COME HOME TO ROOST

The dollar has lubricated international deals in everything from oil to wicker baskets, and most nations hold their reserve funds in dollar-denominated assets. Indeed, they have little choice if they want to buy or sell oil. The Organization of Petroleum Exporting Countries (OPEC) agreed back in 1971, when the world jettisoned the gold standard, to trade its oil in dollars, making the U.S. currency the de facto major international trading currency. Forced to hoard dollars for international oil trading, nations around the world have used their dollar holdings for other trade, too. In recent years, many of the dollars churned out in trade have been coming back to us. For one thing, the Asian financial crisis of 1997–98 caused a "flight to quality" in the United States. Foreigners have used their dollars to buy up hard assets like American real estate and stock in our corporations. They also buy our Treasury bonds—in effect, lending our dollars back to us so we can keep right on indulging our extravagant spending habits. But the large inflows of foreign capital carry a more immediate price tag: the outflow of still more dollars to pay foreigners the interest, dividends, and profits they earn on their investments, thereby increasing the overall trade deficit.

Americans are hooked on credit. In all, the nation's debt—individual, corporate, and government—adds up to $22.4 trillion, more than *twice* the value of everything the economy produced last year! Household debt has tripled in a single generation, accounting for 42 percent of the total. Businesses have borrowed about a third of it, and government debt makes up the other 25 percent. Because savings are so low, there isn't enough capital accumulating in our economy to finance all the available investment opportunities. So we rely on foreign lenders, who last year furnished one-third of our $1.7 trillion in net borrowing.

In addition, foreigners now hold $1.5 trillion of all federal government debt in public hands. Its growth in recent years has been mind-boggling. From only $14 billion in 1970, the total of U.S. debt held by foreigners jumped to $440 billion by 1990 and nearly doubled to $800 billion by 1995, before soaring to its present peak.

Foreign investors have been spending more than $1 billion every business day to buy our federal bonds and notes, and another $1 billion a day to buy up American assets. In all, foreigners now hold about 12 percent of the U.S. stock market, 23 percent of our corporate bonds, and nearly 40 percent of all our Treasury bonds and notes. Back in 1992, only 18 percent of our government's publicly held debt was in foreign hands.

The consequences of this are far from abstract. On one level, the enormous trade deficit represents cash money leaving our control—$489 billion last year. That is money we could have used to improve U.S. education, to shore up homeland security, to repair our highways, or to balance the federal budget and pay down the unprecedented and dangerous level of national debt. Foreigners use the trade deficit to buy *our* assets, and when they lend our money back to us, we have to pay them interest, *more* money that can't be used for our own purposes. On another level, our risky behavior is made worse by how we use the foreign capital. The borrowings used to finance cur-

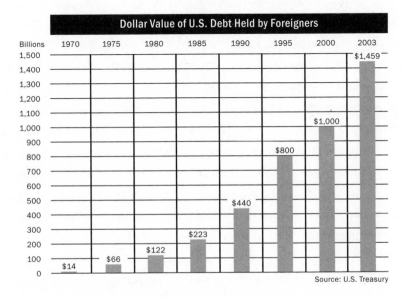

Source: U.S. Treasury

rent consumption and federal budget deficits, rather than productive investment, simply mortgage our children's future.

THE REAL WEAPON OF MASS DESTRUCTION

Without foreign investors, the United States would be bankrupt today. Without the $2 billion or so they send us every business day, we would have to tighten our belts and live far more frugally. Nonetheless, we must recognize that we are depending on the kindness of foreign strangers. It is a dependence that is fraught with danger. Our large and growing foreign debt threatens our status and authority around the world. The agenda of our foreign creditors is often not our agenda. Their interests and ours do not always coincide. Being the world's largest debtor nation jeopardizes our standing in world councils and hands greater potential political and economic leverage to other governments. How they choose to use their large dollar holdings could cripple the U.S. economy—and threats to do so may already be affecting our political decisions.

The problem—and the peril—is that foreigners are getting tired of supporting us. Foreign investors—governments primarily—are becoming nervous about our ability to repay our debt. They see America's spending as out of control: Our budget deficit has exploded under President Bush; our trade deficit has increased steadily over the last decade under Presidents Clinton and Bush. And debt of all kinds—corporate and personal—has risen inexorably. In addition, foreign investors lost a great deal of money in the stock-market collapse that followed the bursting of the dot-com bubble, and now our current low interest rates are making our Treasury bonds less attractive.

Unfortunately, there is a growing distrust of America internationally. Many foreign investors disapprove of the way the United States bullied other nations over Iraq and ultimately went to war virtually on its own. They believe that our dependence on oil and our fear of losing our grip on world trade played no small part in our decision to go to war. I truly hope history proves them wrong.

All these negatives are taking a toll. Last year, new foreign investment in the United States was only a tenth of what it was in 2000. Some investors have obviously cut back or stopped buying altogether. Increasingly, those foreign investors that are still buying are putting their money not into long-term investments, but into stocks and notes that can be unloaded quickly if the economy sours.

If the situation deteriorates, they will demand higher interest rates to buy more of our Treasury bonds and notes. Today, the interest rates on our government securities are at historic lows. As I pointed out in Chapter 5, a sharp rise would be a *disaster.* Long before rates rose to the level at which all the revenues of the federal Treasury would be consumed, we would be forced to default—printing worthless money to pay the interest, thus sending the dollar into a free fall.

Moreover, if foreign investors become worried enough to begin dumping back onto the market the bonds they already hold, they could start a run on the Treasury. That would be catastrophic—both for the United States and the world. Interest rates would rise dramatically, the value of the dollar would plunge, and the global economy would be strangled.

All this explains why our trade deficit has been called the world economy's biggest flaw, one that could threaten *global* prosperity. The International Monetary Fund warned in 2003 that our foreign debt could soon reach 40 percent of our total economy—"an unprecedented level of external debt for a large industrial country." It is a level of debt that could devastate global finance, hampering investment and economic growth around the world.

Other nations have accepted dollars as an international currency because of our excellent credit history, and also because the OPEC trade agreement gave them little choice. Nevertheless, past experience made them trust that the United States would stand behind its currency and maintain its value. The stability of the major currencies is what makes world trade possible. If other nations lose their trust in the dollar, however—if they come to fear that our government and its economy are weakening and that we won't or can't do anything to stem the decline in the valuation of the dollar—they will stop doing business in the dollar, and its value will crumble.

Since the early 1970s, when the dollar was cut loose from its gold backing, thus averting a global monetary crisis, the dollar has itself been the global currency standard. It has been the trading vehicle and reserve currency for most nations; wealthy foreigners bought assets denominated in dollars as an insurance policy against upheavals in their own countries. The ready availability of dollar funds in international markets and our relatively high rate of productivity and low rate of inflation made such investments very attractive.

From being depressed in the late 1970s, the dollar was up 80 percent against other currencies in the 1980s. After tumbling again by the end of the decade, it soared to new heights in the 1990s. However, since 2000, the dollar has lost an astonishing 28 percent of its value against foreign currencies. No one talks about the "almighty dollar" anymore.

Even a slowly depreciating dollar can spur global inflation, as evidenced by OPEC's recent actions. Because OPEC pegs the price of oil in dollars, the dollar's decline last year cut sharply into the oil-producing nations' buying power. Early in 2004, they reacted by curbing production enough to raise crude oil prices to near-record levels, thus pushing up energy prices around the world. That is why gasoline now costs more than $2 a gallon at most American pumps.

A falling dollar should have some trade advantages for Americans. For one thing, it should discourage imports to the United States because foreign goods become more expensive to U.S. consumers. We have to hand over more of our dollars to pay for goods in the exporting country's currency. By the same token, a cheaper dollar should help exports because they become less expensive in foreign markets. The foreign buyers have to exchange less of their currency to get the dollars to buy our goods. But, in recent years, our supposed advantage has come to naught. American consumers' appetites for imported goods have yet to slacken, despite the higher prices, and a sluggish global economy has restrained the purchase of U.S.-made goods abroad.

But even if a weaker dollar does help the trade balance over time, it poses an enormous risk as long as we depend so heavily on foreign lenders. As the dollar falls, the interest we pay foreigners is worth less in their own currencies, and the dollars we use to repay them will be worth less when their U.S. bonds mature. They are sure to demand higher interest rates to offset their losses. Again, if the dollar continues to decline, it raises the chance that foreigners may cash in their Treasury notes and bonds and exchange their dollar holdings for Japanese yen, British pounds, or euros. That could trigger a panic, as investors try to unload their dollars at bargain-basement prices, forcing a catastrophic plunge in the dollar. This is exactly what happened to Argentina in 2002.

If that were to happen, says well-known money manager Dean LeBaron, the euro would probably be the weapon of mass destruction that does us in. Like many a banana republic, we would have to ratchet up interest rates still higher to try to entice lenders. The value of both dollars and Treasury securities would sink, and inflation triggered by the plunging dollar—already up to its highest level in years—would ravage our economy. A vicious cycle would set in, as foreigners stepped up to buy our remaining assets at fire-sale prices in terms of their strong currencies. Inflation would roar, interest rates would rise into the stratosphere and stay there, and economic activity would grind to a halt, bringing on another Great Depression. Furthermore, the toppling of the U.S. economy would almost surely decimate the world economy, too, for we have been the biggest player for years. There would be no safe refuge for people's money—which is one reason the IMF is so concerned.

There are several strong forces working against this scenario. For one, large-scale conversions of dollar assets to euros would make the euro much more expensive, damping down Europe's exports and its whole economy. Nor is the Federal Reserve powerless. It could head off calamity by tightening monetary policy to engineer a lower current-account balance. But the rebalancing would likely prove bumpy for the United States, causing substantial declines in GDP and increased joblessness. At present, as the dollar continues to slide, foreign lenders get hammered with losses every day. At some point, they will have to start selling.

America's budget and trade deficits are an explosive combination. As they continue to pile up, the dollars multiplying in foreign hands are becoming a glut on the market (the reason behind the dollar's fall since 2000). Able to get higher or safer returns in other currencies, foreign investors sell their dollars at a discount, further accelerating the decline. Middle Eastern investors, angry over America's invasion of Iraq, have already pulled billions of dollars out of U.S. investments and dumped them onto the market. In February of 2004, *The Wall Street Journal* reported that Asian central banks, too, were looking at alternatives to dollar-denominated investments. China and Japan hold hundreds of billions of dollar assets. The Japanese government has been a huge buyer, propping up the U.S. currency to prevent its own yen from climbing too high and crimping Japanese exports. If one Asian central bank decided to lessen its dollar holdings, others might well rush to follow. It wouldn't take much to provoke a full-fledged run on the dollar.

The international role of the dollar and the strength and size of our economy make the United States a special case among nations, allowing it to sustain trade deficits at somewhat higher levels than other countries. But make no mistake: The trade deficit has us walking a high wire without a net. Reverses in Iraq, another terrorist attack, or worsening economic news at home could be enough to trigger a major dollar sell-off.

Because of the size of our enormous debt and trade deficit, the United States is like a runaway train headed for a collision, with the engineer standing frozen at the controls. America's trade deficits could trigger a rapid escalation in interest rates. With our enormous debt—growing bigger by the day—a significant rise in interest rates would be catastrophic, consuming an ever-increasing amount of our tax revenues to make payments on the debt. Our twin deficits—trade and budget—are a real and present danger to us and our way of life and to the world at large. No one can predict the point where concern tips into panic, resulting in a major sell-off of the dollar and a sudden rise in interest rates. But if it happens, it will be hard to reverse.

Unless we slash our annual deficits, and quickly reverse course on our escalating debt, our economy is a train wreck waiting to happen.

CHAPTER 7

SOCIAL INSECURITY

IF YOU ARE 39 as you read these words, you're not even close to middle age. Owing to incredible advances in health care, you may live decades longer than your grandparents. By 2050, when you reach 85, you'll be part of the fastest-growing age group in the United States. That's the good news.

The bad is that you might be almost totally broke. With no company pension (canceled years ago), and little left in your 401(k), you're likely to experience shrinking Social Security checks, few doctors who will accept Medicare fees, and so little cash that barter will become a way of life. Worst of all, you may be chained to the same efficiency apartment or to the mobile home in which you drove to Florida 20 years before in search of sun and solitude. Your mobile home will likely be surrounded by scores of other trailers inhabited by fellow marooned octogenarians unable to pick up stakes and travel elsewhere. To make ends meet, you may have to compete for scarce jobs, flipping burgers at McDonald's at three bucks an hour, down from four bucks an hour several years previous. The aged burger flippers wearing those funny hats won't feel funny, just cheated.

Welcome to "trailer park nation," the dark future our leaders are steering us toward. This is not your parents' old age, when corporate pensions and Social Security evoked visions of guaranteed freedom, a well-earned beginning of the rest of your life.

No, this is the flip side of that future, when 80-year-olds brimming with health may find themselves scrounging for rent money. All because Social Security by then will have been driven into destitution by our elected leaders through a vast pyramid scheme that makes swindler Charles Ponzi look like a piker.

The Social Security trust fund is a travesty, a Potemkin village filled with potentially worthless U.S. Treasury bonds. As I revealed earlier in the book, the current surplus in payroll and employer taxes that might provide for future beneficiaries is routinely raided by the government to pay for other federal expenses. Former Treasury Secretary Paul O'Neill upset a lot of people in the Bush Administration by telling the truth—that the Social Security trust fund has no tangible assets. It's empty. So where does that leave us? What's the patient's prognosis?

For the next few years, although Social Security has no cash in its fund, the income it receives from today's workers is more than sufficient to pay the benefits for today's retirees. In 2003, payroll tax deductions brought in an estimated $631.9 billion, while paying out an estimated $479.1 billion in benefits. The balance was "loaned" to the federal government, which issued nontransferable bonds (valueless IOUs).

But all that is about to change dramatically. The patient's prognosis: very poor.

To start with, the number of retirees is about to explode. The oldest baby boomers, those born in 1946, are just four years away from early retirement and eight years from being able to retire with full benefits at age 66. When America's largest generation begins to clock out of the working world in 2008, fewer wage earners will be left to provide the benefits for this sudden bulge of retirees. The annual fund surpluses will begin to shrink. In 2002, the United States had 3.3 workers to support every person aged 65 or older. By 2030, the ratio is expected to drop to 2.2 workers per retiree. And the ratio of workers to retirees will continue a gradual decline for the rest of the century. That's a sure formula for disaster.

What's more, demographers predict that the baby boomers will live far longer and collect Social Security checks for many more years than their parents. Americans' life expectancy today is 78 years and

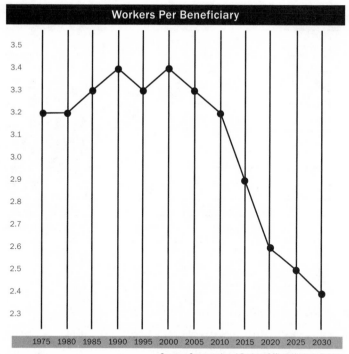

Source: Congressional Budget Office. Historic Tables

rising. More and more of the 85-and-older crowd will pass the century mark. The numbers of these elder senior citizens will expand from just 4 million in 1998 to an expected 40 million by 2050.

As fewer and fewer workers pay for more and more retirees, the system will stop booking surpluses altogether, probably in 2017. That's when the government will have to start forking over its own money to cover the fund deficit and begin redeeming its IOUs.

Not only will the federal government lose the surplus money it now spends, it will have to fork over additional revenues. Inevitably, a new way of financing benefits will have to be found, or the size of payroll deductions will have to be substantially increased. But even higher payroll tax deductions would be merely a stopgap measure. As greater numbers retire, Social Security will sink further into the red, and the government will need more and more cash to make good on its promised benefits.

The highly respected Concord Coalition speculates that the run-up to a Social Security crisis might look like this:

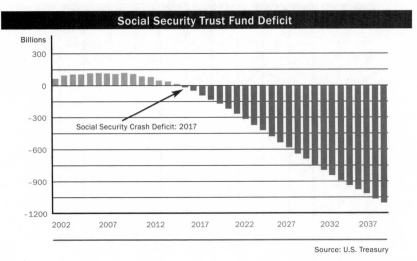

Social Security Trust Fund Deficit

Billions

Social Security Crash Deficit: 2017

Source: U.S. Treasury

1. In 2008, the program's annual cash surplus starts to shrink.
2. In 2017, cash outflows exceed cash inflows. Social Security turns from a cash cow to a fiscal liability. The federal government not only loses a source of funds with which to bankroll defense, education, roads, and other programs, it has to come up with additional money to pay retirees. This is when the first major Social Security crisis will hit.
3. From 2017 through 2041, the government will have to find revenue to make good on all the nonmarketable bonds, or IOUs, it was pouring into the Social Security trust fund when it was hijacking the cash for other uses.
4. By 2041, the trust assets will be depleted, leaving Social Security with enough incoming tax receipts to pay just 73 percent of benefits. To return that 73 percent to 100 percent would require a 34 percent payroll tax hike. As of 2041, the cost of financing Social Security alone will consume 6.7 percent of the nation's economic output, topping even the Pentagon as the federal government's single biggest expense. For the 30-somethings of today, this is *your* Social Security I am talking about. And this constitutes the second major Social Security crisis.

Looking at this scenario, you may be tempted to say—as our leaders have said out loud for years—"What? Me worry? We've got years to figure it out, right?"

Wrong. The time frame I've just sketched out is based on a statistical analysis. It doesn't factor in the political realities, which are sure to put Social Security under the gun within the next few years.

Once the Social Security cash surplus begins to shrink in 2008, the government will be desperate to find more cash to fund expenditures. By that point, given today's deficits, the federal debt will be so gigantic, and interest payments on that debt so huge, that the government will almost certainly be constrained from borrowing more. Its only option will be to choke off its voracious appetite for cash. And where do you think the chokehold will be applied first? On two of the biggest money guzzlers in the budget: Social Security and Medicare.

How did we get into this mess? Didn't our representatives in Congress notice that America's two major entitlement programs were in imminent danger of collapse? That our future obligations had no cash deposits to back them? That Congress and our presidents were stealing from the Social Security piggy bank, and at some point the bill would come due?

Sure they did. But terrified of addressing the problem and potentially stirring up animosity among the senior-citizen voter bloc, our larcenous Congress averted its eyes and kept on siphoning off surplus cash from the trust fund, replacing it with worthless IOUs. It simply couldn't afford to ruffle the feathers of this golden goose. And so, year after year, the centerpieces of the New Deal and the Great Society, conceived with such grand promise, have drifted closer and closer to insolvency.

A TWISTED PATH

Launched by President Franklin Roosevelt in 1935 during the Great Depression, Social Security was originally envisioned as a trust fund limited to providing workers with modest but guaranteed pensions when they retired at age 65. Though common in Europe, a social insurance program was revolutionary in the United States. It was truly a New Deal for a battered nation.

At first, Social Security was a real trust fund, immune to invasion by free-spending politicians. Financed by means of a payroll tax—initially 2 percent of a worker's income and a matching amount from each employer—workers' savings-via-taxes were literally held in trust and invested for growth. In essence, the government was forcing people to save for old age; in return, it paid a fair rate of interest on the accumulating nest egg. But in 1939, only four years into the program, the trust fund was converted into a pay-as-you-go plan that paid benefits to an older generation of retirees with tax dollars contributed by the current generation of workers. Benefits were based on years worked, income earned, and Social Security taxes paid.

The move to pay-as-you-go represented a profound change. Instead of setting aside the dollars a worker paid in for his or her own retirement, the government was now sending much of the money right back out the door to finance some older fellow's pension, using Peter's money to pay Paul. It seemed like a pretty good way to do things at the time. There were many more workers than retirees—the ratio was about 45 to 1—and who knew then that Americans would have fewer and fewer children as the years went by—or that Americans would live longer and longer. In 1940, only 40 percent of the workforce reached retirement age. The idea that someday there might be too few workers to support too many retirees was not on anyone's radar screen.

With so many more workers than retirees back then, the Social Security payroll taxes generally brought in far more funds than were needed to cover current benefits. The extra income was theoretically put into a trust fund. In reality, the surplus dollars were too tempting to a cash-hungry government. The trust fund became an accounting convention used to keep track of the Social Security tax receipts and spending. The government swiped the actual cash, put it into its general revenue pot, and spent it, while making bookkeeping entries for claims on the Treasury that would be redeemed as needed. In effect, the Social Security trust fund was filled with Treasury IOUs. Worse yet, because the money was "borrowed" from Social Security, the money the government spent didn't get added to the annual deficit reported to the public. In essence, it allowed the government to hide tens of billions of dollars of additional deficits.

Charged with paying for the day-to-day necessities of government and unable to restrain its penchant for big new spending programs larded with generous portions of pork, Congress found it all too tempting to move those excess dollars from the Social Security ledger—called "borrowings," of course—onto the overall budget rolls to hide the politicians' fiscal failures. While employers are required by law to safeguard their employees' pensions, the Social Security trust fund had no such protection. Our leaders simply commandeered the fund's assets and spent them, adding new bookkeeping entries to represent interest paid in the form of more Treasury IOUs. In short order, a major swindle was under way, and the future of Social Security was put in jeopardy.

Social Security's history has been a long-running drama of politicians steadily adding new beneficiaries and benefits to the system while simultaneously stealing the surpluses for other government programs and ignoring the consequences. Roosevelt's original idea limited Social

Cumulative Cash Taken from the Social Security Trust Fund

Billions	1982	1984	1986	1988	1990	1992	1994	1996	1998	2000	2002	2004
	$19	$36	$45	$104	$214	$314	$422	$550	$730	$1,007	$1,329	$1,484

Source: Social Security Trust Fund Data, December 30, 2003

Security to those who spent their lives working in business and industry. Later, Social Security was amended to allow people with only five years of covered employment to qualify for benefits. Yep—all a person had to do to start drawing a lifelong check from the government was to work a mere 260 weeks. What a bonanza that turned out to be for military and other government workers who were not required to pay into the Social Security system. They could retire after 20 years with their own excellent pension benefits, then enter the civilian workforce and pay into the system for a few short years, which permitted them to retire with Social Security benefits, as well, double- or triple-dipping from the Treasury for the rest of their lives.

All too typically, Congress gave without first figuring out how to pay. No actuarial reserves were set aside to cover these new expenses or a host of other changes: the 1939 addition of retirees' dependents and survivors, the 1957 addition of disabled persons, the 1966 addition of Medicare and Medicaid as Social Security obligations, and the 1972 inclusion of cost-of-living allowances (COLAs) to help retirees offset the impact of inflation on their pensions. The Social Security system—now officially known as Old Age and Survivors Insurance (OASI) to cover all its beneficiaries—began running deficits that had to be financed, in part, from the general revenues. In 1968, Washington belatedly moved to remedy the situation by imposing higher payroll taxes, thereby raising the joint contributions of employers and employees to 8 percent of workers' annual earnings. But the new taxes barely covered the new benefit packages that were being extended to an ever-larger group of recipients.

Don't misunderstand me. Social Security greatly improved life for millions of poor and middle-class Americans. That achievement can't be dismissed or begrudged. The number of elderly Americans living below the poverty line was cut in half between 1959 and 1990. The paradox of this undeniable force for good is that Congress launched and expanded it with such dim understanding and foresight of the potential trouble spots ahead that, eventually, the survival of the entire program was threatened. By 1982, the Social Security surplus had fallen for seven straight years. With no actuarial reserve in hand, more was being paid out in benefits than the system received in payroll taxes. It was fast going broke.

What to do?

Our politicians rode to the rescue as they always do. In 1983, President Reagan appointed a commission, and Washington crossed its fingers that its members would concoct the least painful remedy (for the politicians, that is, who didn't want to trim any benefits and then have to face angry retirees at the polls). Sure enough, the Social Security commission, chaired by Alan Greenspan, recommended the easiest (and worst) solution possible: still-higher payroll taxes without any guaranteed long-term funding of the program. Instead of a pay-as-you-go system in which each working generation supported the preceding generation of retirees, current workers now would be expected to pay for current retirees and also pay in advance for the rising costs of a growing population of future retirees. But the plan's biggest flaw was that the funds collected were still not protected from sticky-fingered politicians.

In 1983, Congress converted the Greenspan recommendations into law, and the raise-the-payroll-tax solution took on a life of its own. By 1990, the tax had soared to 15.3 percent on the first $55,200 in income. Furthermore, retirees with incomes in excess of $25,000 (or $32,000 for couples) were obliged to hand back 50 percent of their Social Security benefits to the government. The 50 percent giveback was eliminated a few years later for people over the age of 65. But the government came up with another sneaky way of squeezing retirees: Social Security benefits were redefined as earned income and taxed. Thus, wage earners, who pay the Social Security taxes into the system in the first place, are now taxed a second time when the money comes back to them in the form of benefits. This is institutionalized double-dipping on a grand scale.

Senator Daniel Patrick Moynihan of New York called the 1983 amendment to the Social Security law a "robbery." Senator John Heinz of Pennsylvania described it as more of an embezzlement.

Moynihan made a much-publicized effort to keep the government's hand out of the Social Security cookie jar—to no avail.

The sponsors of the 1983 law assured the country that Social Security was now fixed, forever. They claimed that the huge tax increase would pile up enormous surpluses, guaranteeing ample pension money to cover the deluge of aging baby boomers just visible on the far horizon. But it was all a cruel hoax. Between 1983 and early 2004, $1.8 trillion in extra revenues *was* collected. But was that money tucked safely away to pay benefits when the floodgates opened, spilling retired boomers across the landscape? Of course not. Like every other trust-fund dollar collected by the government, the cash was stolen—"borrowed" to fund part of the annual federal budget deficit. If a corporation had pulled this stunt, the missing money would represent an unfunded liability, and it would have to face the music. But Congress only makes the laws—it doesn't necessarily follow them. Our leaders effectively absconded with the money, helped by a little imaginative accounting, thereby masking the real size of the annual spending deficit.

THE CON GAME

Unlike public companies, which operate under the accrual accounting method and have to recognize expenses and revenues as soon as they're incurred or earned, the government uses cash-basis accounting. Cash accounting allows you to put off recording income and expenses until the money actually changes hands. So whereas companies have to put aside reserves for things they know they're going to have to pay in the future, the government can totally forget about any long-term debts—like the promises it's made to Social Security beneficiaries—until the bills actually come due. Meanwhile, it can go on spending wildly and allow program costs to balloon as if the well of revenues were bottomless.

This willful state of amnesia meant that the Social Security Administration could report a 2003 surplus of $161 billion, when, in fact, accrual accounting, factoring in Social Security obligations, would have shown that the system actually had a loss for the year. Simply put, Social Security has assets of $3.5 trillion, which includes payroll taxes plus the amount kept in the so-called trust funds filled with nonnegotiable U.S. Treasury bonds. But it is committed to paying $14 trillion to future beneficiaries. The gap between those assets and liabilities widened by $370 billion last year alone and now totals $10.5 trillion.

In the following table, you can see for yourself how the rape of the Social Security program has played out year by year. Column 1 indicates what the system receives in payroll tax receipts each year. Column 2 shows what the system pays out in benefits and operating expenses each year. Column 3 lists the annual surplus (income minus outgo) that could have been (but was not) put aside in an inviolable trust fund to cover the system's deficit. Column 4 shows the trust fund's theoretical assets in the form of nonnegotiable U.S. bonds. You'll see that, for

Updated December 2003

Fiscal Year Trust Fund Operations (in Millions)

Year	Total Receipts	Total Expenditures	Net increase during year	Amount at end of year
1982	$148,028	$155,964	−$7,936	$19,290
1983	$170,280	$170,058	+$12,660	$31,950
1984	$178,461	$178,199	$262	$32,212
1985	$197,865	$188,504	$7,538	$39,750
1986	$215,461	$198,730	$6,117	$45,867
1987	$226,893	$207,323	$19,570	$65,437
1988	$258,090	$219,290	$38,800	$104,237
1989	$284,936	$232,491	$52,445	$156,682
1990	$306,822	$248,605	$58,217	$214,900
1991	$322,611	$269,096	$53,515	$268,415
1992	$338,270	$287,524	$50,746	$319,161
1993	$351,354	$304,566	$46,788	$365,949
1994	$376,307	$319,551	$56,757	$422,706
1995	$396,276	$335,830	$60,446	$483,152
1996	$416,064	$349,654	$66,410	$549,562
1997	$446,553	$365,238	$81,316	$630,878
1998	$478,608	$379,291	$99,318	$730,195
1999	$514,731	$390,019	$124,712	$854,908
2000	$561,251	$409,404	$151,847	$1,006,754
2001	$595,913	$432,929	$162,987	$1,169,741
2002	$614,977	$455,910	$159,067	$1,328,808
2003	$630,253	$474,721	$155,532	$1,484,340

Source: OASDI Trust Fund Data, 2004

two decades, the stolen surpluses have steadily grown year by year, in step with the rising paper value of the trust fund. By the end of 2003, the trust fund had increased to a make-believe value of $1.48 trillion, and our future obligations are trillions of dollars higher yet.

Can we fix such a seemingly hopeless situation? Yes—but we must act quickly. The longer we wait, the more pain will be incurred to fix the system.

PRESCRIPTIONS

Experts have suggested all sorts of fixes for the Social Security mess. Among them:

- Increase payroll taxes. An across-the-board increase could build up the trust fund, assuming Congress and the President didn't spend it. But given our government's 60-year history with Social Security, that's a very big assumption. It would also put a heavy burden on workers. The payroll tax rate already stands at a steep 15.3 percent, without providing any long-term fix. And, at present, it falls heaviest on lower-income Americans. One approach might be to make *all* wages subject to a payroll tax. Today, all income above $87,900 is exempt from Social Security taxes (the Medicare tax does not have an income limit), making it a highly regressive tax that gives high-income families a largely free ride.
- Curtail COLAs. At present, benefits are raised in sync with the consumer price index. Because the CPI is based on prices, many believe that it overstates the rate of inflation. Trimming the cost-of-living adjustment, as Alan Greenspan recently suggested, would more closely align benefit increases with the true rate of inflation.
- Begin paying benefits later. Reacting to Americans' increased longevity, Congress is gradually raising the age at which full benefits can be claimed from 65 to 67 for those born in 1960 or later. We can speed up the phase-in process and raise the retirement age by another year or two. Or even three, if necessary.

- Privatize. Instead of sending workers' Social Security payroll deductions to Washington, allow workers to put some or all of the payments into investment vehicles that would provide higher yields. Social Security takes huge amounts of potential savings that could be invested in stocks and bonds, creating new jobs and a stronger economy. We currently pay an enormous penalty in lost opportunities for growth.

- Tighten our belts. Let the level of benefits slide down to 73 percent in the future, or to whatever level the payroll tax would support. I admit that such a drop would wreak havoc for millions of Americans on fixed incomes. But it would send the nation a sure signal that we can no longer meet all of our commitments to our citizens.

Probably none of the suggested fixes by themselves could rescue Social Security as we know it. Without a firm bipartisan commitment to stop our crippling deficit spending and start building up the Social Security reserves, only one serious option remains: Expenditures will have to be slashed. And because the entitlement programs eat up so much of the budget, that is where the ax will surely fall.

What's needed is a national retirement system that we can trust to invest our savings wisely and provide us with sufficient income to live reasonably well in our retirement years. It would need to incorporate an unbreakable lockbox that protects our savings from being appropriated by Congress or the President to finance our government's current excesses. We actually have such a system in the form of individual retirement accounts (IRAs), and it works. Millions of Americans already use them to invest their savings without paying taxes on the gains for withdrawals made after the age of 59. When cash is later withdrawn—participants must begin withdrawing cash from the accounts at age 70—it's taxed as ordinary income. Contributions are tax-deductible, too, as long as you fall under certain income limits.

The beauty of the IRA is that holders can invest in bonds, stocks, or any other legal private market they choose. And unlike the money we pay into Social Security, U.S. Treasury raiders can't touch it.

The drawback at this juncture is that IRAs are not treated on a par with Social Security in terms of tax benefits. You can deduct up to $3,000 in IRA contributions per year from your taxes in 2004, $4,000 per year in 2005 through 2007, and $5,000 in 2008. And if you exceed the limits, you can be fined 6 percent of the excess. Self-employed people can get a better break using the Keogh tax-deferred savings plan (named after the senator who invented it), which allows much higher deductible contributions. But neither IRAs nor Keoghs are currently sufficient to replace Social Security.

The other retirement savings vehicle that has grown dramatically in importance is the employer-sponsored 401(k), which allows employees to set aside up to $13,000 of their 2004 salaries in tax-deferred investment accounts. The limit is scheduled to increase by $1,000 a year until it hits $15,000 in 2006. People aged 50 and older may also be allowed to make extra "catch-up" contributions of $3,000, with the maximum increasing to $5,000 by 2006. Many employers match part or all of an employee's contribution, a company perk that offers a tremendous incentive to increase one's saving up to the level of the company match.

Both contributions and income earned in a 401(k) are nontaxable until the funds are withdrawn. And since withdrawals generally are made after retirement, the tax rate is typically lower than what you would have paid otherwise. But a 401(k) is not without risk, depending on the type of investment you choose for your money. Many people lost money in their 401(k)s following the collapse of the stock-market bubble. Beware of plans that encourage you to invest most or all of your contribution in your employer's stock. That leaves you with both salary and savings dependent on your company's business environment and your boss's decisions. Enron's and WorldCom's former employees lost both their retirement nest eggs and their jobs when management's misdeeds were discovered.

At this writing, various savings options have been proposed by the Bush Administration to encourage Americans to save. So far, none has made it through Congress. These include:

- Lifetime Savings Accounts, which would carry no tax advantage for contributions, but earnings would be tax-free. They could be used for any purpose, not just retirement.
- Retirement Savings Accounts, which would allow after-tax contributions up to $5,000 a year; investors could accumulate earnings tax-free in an RSA account and could use the money for retirement without having to pay additional taxes.
- Employer Retirement Savings Accounts, which would consolidate and simplify employer-based plans like the 401(k) and 403(b); the tax advantage on an ERSA account would be identical to the plan it replaced.

A MEDICAL EMERGENCY

Our present Social Security mess is a self-inflicted wound that will not heal itself. No one wants to revisit the days when old age for many citizens meant almost certain poverty. No one wants to live in a trailer park nation. But that is what will happen if we don't fix Social Security once and for all and stop Congress's destruction of our social safety net.

Social Security, however, is far from the only gathering cloud over the future of our aging population. The same demographics and the same fiscal theft perpetrated by our politicians threaten Medicare, too. Only, in this instance, skyrocketing medical costs are conspiring to turn an egregious situation into a desperate one far more quickly. In the next chapter, I'll spell out the details of our nation's medical emergency.

CHAPTER 8

ADDING INJURY TO INJURY

Shall I eat lunch today or take my heart medication?

Do I cut my blood-pressure tablet in half to save money, even though my doctor has warned that I could suffer a stroke?

If I could afford to have these cataracts removed, I could drive again and get out and about with my friends instead of spending day after lonely day cooped up in this apartment.

IMAGINE A WORLD in which *your* elderly mother or father has to choose between food and medicine because she or he can't afford both.

A world in which ordinary Americans can't hope to come up with the money to pay the exorbitant costs of even relatively minor medical procedures.

Wait a minute, you say. My parents aren't poor. They're middle-class Americans with a little retirement savings to supplement their Social Security, and Medicare to pay for prescription drugs, medical procedures, and hospital care.

Sure, I realize Social Security might be broke when I retire. But my parents' medical benefits are safe, aren't they? After all, President Bush and Congress just passed a prescription drug benefit in 2003.

I'm here to tell you your parents' benefits *aren't* safe. And, ironically, that prescription-drug benefit the President signed with so much fanfare has put Americans—senior citizens, the middle-aged, and young people alike—in more immediate danger than ever before. Billions of dollars of new spending for prescription drugs, in the backwash of the trillions of dollars of revenues lost to the Bush tax cuts, is the kind of math that leads to disaster.

This headline from my morning paper says it all:

"MEDICARE BANKRUPT IN 15 YEARS. Benefits Reduced After 2010."

Sounds like a headline from my doomsday account of the Ringers back in Chapter 2, doesn't it?

Except that this calamitous warning comes from the trustees of the Medicare trust fund. The news from their annual report to Congress? It's all bad. The projected date of total insolvency for the Medicare fund that pays hospital benefits has leaped forward by seven years since last year's report. It is now projected to run out of reserves in 2019. Worse yet, the fund will actually begin running deficits this year, as hospital spending exceeds payroll tax revenues. The crisis is right on our doorstep, not 10 years down the road as was forecast as recently as 2003.

And hospitalization isn't the only aspect of Medicare that's in trouble. The program that covers doctors' fees and outpatient services is in dire straits, too. Financed by general budget revenues, it will also feel the squeeze of reduced tax receipts. Mincing no words, the trustees flatly state that the entire list of Medicare entitlements is doomed without some sort of congressional fix.

None of this comes as a surprise. A year ago, when the hospital fund was still expected to be solvent until 2026, the trustees urged "effective and decisive" funding reforms to stave off the crisis. So what did President Bush and Congress do? They loaded on *more* Medicare spending, including a pie-in-the-sky prescription-drug benefit, with *no provision at all for meeting the costs.* Those costs, disclosed only *after* the Medicare bill passed, will amount to $534 billion in the bill's first 10 years (not the $400 billion figure the Bush Administration deceptively advertised), and up to *$1 trillion* in the next 10.

NOBLE VISION, IGNOBLE FUNDING

When he signed the Medicare bill into law back in 1965, President Lyndon Johnson expressed its lofty aim: "No longer will young families see their own incomes, and their own hopes, eaten away simply because they are carrying out their deep moral obligation to their parents." What he didn't tell us was that the bill's jerry-built funding structure all but guaranteed that the hopes and incomes of our children and grandchildren would be eroded by the growing burden of taxes needed to keep its promises.

Designed to help the country's senior citizens and the disabled pay medical expenses, Medicare has always been an actuary's nightmare. And funding for Medicaid, the medical program for the poor, is in even worse condition. Many economists believe the vast problems facing these programs make the Social Security mess seem almost simple by comparison. Former U.S. Treasury Secretary Peter G. Peterson points out that there are humane ways to fix Social Security, but "I have yet to see a proposal for Medicare [and Medicaid] reform that truly confronts the magnitude of what looms ahead."

Two devastating facts underlie the coming Medicare fiasco. One is a now-familiar demographic: The first wave of the huge baby-boom generation will begin retiring in 2008—and the longer those 77 million boomers live, the more Medicare benefits they will claim. That's when the second factor really kicks in: Medical costs are rising much faster than prices in general. The combination guarantees that Medicare costs will mushroom, eating up a continuously swelling portion of shrinking federal revenues.

The Medicare breakdown has been long in the making. From its beginning, it was poorly structured to meet the expanding needs of an aging baby-boom population. Piecemeal financing of a multipart benefits package left this cobbled-together edifice wobbly at best. And when a rapidly aging American population meets skyrocketing medical costs, something's got to give. And it will, and soon. Will benefits be cut? Taxes raised? Eligibility adjusted? Programs privatized? These are the stark choices we are left with after 40 years of high-minded promises and low-grade financial support.

THE FEVERISH RISE OF MEDICARE COSTS

Medicare program expenditures already amount to 2.6 percent of the total gross domestic product (GDP). Using conservative assumptions, the trustees predict that the program will grow to 3.7 percent of GDP in 2010, 7.7 percent in 2035, and nearly 14 percent by 2078. To understand what these numbers mean, let me put it in perspective: *Total* federal income tax receipts have averaged 11 percent of GDP over the past half-century.

Medicare spending is expected to surpass Social Security costs in 2024 and eat up *twice* as much revenue as Social Security by 2078. By that time, Medicare will, by itself, be draining away 70 percent of all federal revenue derived from income taxes each year. (Unfunded Social Security benefits will consume the rest of the tax receipts.)

It's flat-out impossible to run the country if all revenues are needed just to keep these two entitlement programs afloat. It's clear

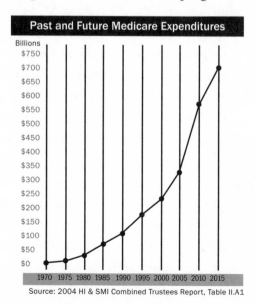

Past and Future Medicare Expenditures

Billions

Source: 2004 HI & SMI Combined Trustees Report, Table II.A1

that some combination of higher taxes, cost controls, and lower benefits will have to be imposed if Medicare is to remain viable. It's equally clear that taking the necessary action will be a political nightmare for whoever is president and for those in Congress who are forced to confront the problem. Their natural instinct, of course, will be to pretend nothing's wrong and hope it will all go away. Unfortunately, even more so than with Social Security, the longer we wait to make changes in the Medicare program, the more painful the solution will become. Skyrocketing health-care costs, multiplied by the expanding Medicare population, will rapidly decimate remaining resources and force ever more Draconian measures to plug the gaps.

SIZING UP MEDICARE PART A: IT'S ENOUGH TO MAKE YOU SICK

To understand the funding problems bedeviling Medicare, you have to understand what each of its parts is supposed to accomplish and the piecemeal ways in which these parts are financed. Let's take it from the top.

Hospital Insurance (HI), also known as Medicare Part A, helps pay for hospital, home health care, skilled nursing facilities, and hospice care. It covers people aged 65 and over, some younger people with disabilities, and patients with permanent kidney failure who must be treated with dialysis or an organ transplant. It is the HI trust fund that faces the most imminent threat to its solvency as outlays begin to exceed income this year.

The HI trust fund is financed largely by payroll taxes, currently 2.9 percent of wages, an amount that is split evenly between employers and employees. After an annual deductible, which was set at $876 for 2004, the trust fund generally pays for all covered services during hospital stays of up to 60 days, and sliding amounts thereafter. Last year, it paid out $24 billion less than it took in, and another surplus was expected for 2004. But higher-than-anticipated expenditures, because of rapidly rising hospital fees, and lower-than-anticipated payroll tax receipts, as a result of slow wage growth, will force the fund to begin drawing down its accumulated surplus this year. In the latest reckoning, that nest egg will totally disappear by 2019, at which point either benefits will have to be trimmed to match revenues or the payroll tax take will have to rise to meet spiraling benefit costs. But the payroll tax will have to keep rising relentlessly as Medicare becomes a larger and larger portion of the national economy. By 2019, payroll taxes at today's rate would cover only 81 percent of expenses. By 2078, they would pay for just 26 percent of the program's costs.

SIZING UP MEDICARE PARTS B AND D: A MIGRAINE IN THE MAKING

The hospital trust fund is the fiscally responsible part of Medicare. Supplementary Medical Insurance (SMI), which encompasses Part B and the newly created Part D, is an open-ended drain on the public purse. Part B pays for doctors' bills, outpatient services, and home health, while Part D will cover the costs of the new Medicare Prescription Drug, Improvement, and Modernization Act of 2003. (Yes, there is a Part C—for coverage available through private managed care plans—which I'll discuss later.)

SMI is supported not by payroll taxes, but by transfers from the general fund of the U.S. Treasury and by premiums from beneficiaries, who currently pay $66.60 a month for Part B, typically as a deduction from their Social Security benefits. Part B carries a $100 annual deductible, after which Medicare pays 80 percent of a beneficiary's doctor bills. The law requires that the monthly premiums cover only 25 percent of actual expenses, with the rest coming out of the Treasury's general fund. In effect, the government has written a blank check, guaranteeing to make up the SMI shortfall no matter how big it becomes. What is more, the Medicare fund, like the Social Security trust fund, is stuffed only with IOUs from the Treasury. When they are redeemed, taxpayers will have to foot the bill. Last year, payments to the SMI trust fund, including interest on the Treasury securities held in the fund, ate up $88.4 billion, or more than 8.7 percent of all federal income tax receipts. By 2040, SMI will swallow an estimated 34 percent of income tax revenues, or an estimated 5 percent of the GDP.

In theory at least, the blank check guarantees that the SMI fund can never run out of money. But the burden on taxpayers inevitably will become backbreaking— particularly now that we're looking at another $1.5 trillion in drug costs over the next 20 years or so. It's futile to look to Medicare recipients to pick up enough of the cost to keep SMI's head above water: Just to hold the program at 25 percent of solvency, the trustees calculate that, after inclusion of the new drug benefit, SMI fees would have to rise from the present 15 percent of the average Social Security benefit to 35 percent in 2010, and to 50 percent by 2030.

Bad as that sounds, these forecasts almost surely understate the reality we face. For one thing, they assume that medical costs will rise only 1 percent faster than general living costs. Recently, medical costs have risen at *three times* that rate. The forecasts also assume continuation of a provision that would reduce the average Medicare fee for doctors' services by 5 percent each year from 2006 to 2012. Doctors are already marshaling themselves to force the repeal of this law, and they'll probably win. But even if the clause were left intact, it would be counterproductive. Medicare patients already scramble to find a doctor among a diminishing number willing to treat them at the restricted rates Medicare pays. If the fees were cut annually in the face of continually rising costs, many more doctors would opt out of the system. Once the part of the law aimed at scaling back doctors' fees dies, as it surely will, Part B costs will be that much higher than the trustees currently predict.

AMERICANS AREN'T GETTING ANY YOUNGER

The Medicare picture grows even bleaker when one factors in the aging American population. Medicare will spend $279 billion this year to serve 41 million clients. But by the time the entire class of 77 million American baby boomers is retired in 2030, Medicare will count a total of 80 million beneficiaries—with declining birth rates leaving fewer active workers contributing taxes to support them. In 1960, there were five workers supporting each retiree. Today, that ratio is 3.3 to 1. By 2030 it will be only 2.2 to 1. In 2075, when children born in this decade are ready for retirement, every two workers will be carrying one pensioner—and they will not relish the load.

Furthermore, retirees are living longer. When Social Security was passed, only 40 percent of the first generation of insured workers reached the age of 65, and those who did lived an average of 13 years more. But 84 percent of the men born in 1985 will reach retirement age, and those pensioners will live on for another 20 years. The older they get, the more medical attention they will need. Consider these medical statistics:

- *Eighty percent of people over 65* have at least one chronic ailment; *nearly two out of three* are so disabled that they need help with daily living.
- A person reaching 65 has a 43 percent chance of needing nursing home care in the future.
- Nearly half of all people over 85 have some degree of dementia— and by 2050, there will be 40 million Americans over 85, 10 times more than there were just five years ago.

All these problems require services that are incredibly expensive. Who will pay for the boomers' enormous medical costs? One way or another, taxpayers will be stuck with those bills—either now or in the future.

MEDICAL COSTS AREN'T GETTING ANY CHEAPER

Medical costs rose 50 percent in the past decade. They rose 9.3 percent in 2002 alone. Over the past 20 years, they've risen an average three percentage points faster than the cost of living. Moreover, the medical market seems uniquely impervious to price competition. For a variety of reasons, someone needing medical treatment seldom bothers to ask what it costs. Furthermore, advancements in technology, which usually work to drive down costs, actually make medicine more expensive: New and complex operations become feasible for a larger number of patients; costly diagnostic procedures uncover more illness at an earlier stage and thus lead to more operations; sophisticated and sometimes wildly expensive new drugs race one another to market; and consumers, bombarded with drug-company advertising, press their doctors to prescribe the latest drugs. All told, the odds are heavily stacked against any significant slowing of the rising cost curve.

Some critics argue that Medicare would be more efficient if it were run largely by private insurers. They say competition would encourage seniors to shop for the best prices and choose variable features from a menu tailored to individual needs. Private insurers got a foot inside the Medicare door in 1997 with the advent of Medicare + Choice (now called Medicare Advantage), or Part C. This variation on Part B allows beneficiaries to pay the same premium but go through regional health maintenance organizations (HMOs) or preferred provider organizations (PPOs). Part C plans usually offer more benefits—including, in some cases, prescription drugs—than basic Medicare Part B offers. The Congressional Budget Office estimates that care delivered under Part C costs about 5 percent less than traditional Medicare. But in 2003, only 11 percent of Medicare clients chose HMOs, down from 16 percent at the program's peak.

High hopes for Part C were shattered by a flawed government payment formula that prompted many HMO and PPO plans to cut benefits or back out of the system completely, leaving participants in the lurch. Not surprisingly, personal experience and news reports about the plight of those people caught up in the fiasco left many seniors wary of the Part C options.

Nonetheless, those in favor of privatizing Medicare hope to expand the principle with a new "premium support" system that allows enrollees to choose between traditional Medicare and a menu of private health plans offering benefits equal to or greater than basic Medicare. The government would kick in a subsidy for each individual, based on the average annual costs of Medicare and the private plans. A beneficiary could also choose a private plan costing more than the subsidy, paying the added premium out of pocket.

The evidence that privatized health care would offer real savings, however, is, at best, mixed. Critics of Medicare Advantage and similar pilot programs argue that savings vary by region, with HMOs actually costing more than Medicare in some localities. They also fear that private plans would cherry-pick healthier retirees whose costs are low, leaving Medicare with the sickest seniors whose rising premiums would drive still more beneficiaries into the private plans.

And whatever their long-term hopes for cost savings from privatization, Congress and the Bush Administration clearly have little faith in the short term. In fact, the Bush Administration's own projections are that managed care will cost more than traditional Medicare for the foreseeable future. The Medicare modernization bill passed last year by the Republican-led Congress and signed by President Bush includes $46 billion in subsidies for private insurers to lure them into the program.

Long term, the best hope for cost relief is a restructuring of the health-care system to deal better with patients' needs, particularly chronic illness. Medicare was designed in the 1960s, when the typical patient was a low-income elderly person hospitalized for surgery. Today's typical high-risk beneficiary is an elderly woman in her eighties with a host of chronic conditions. Several doctors may prescribe medicines, with or without the knowledge of the patient's other providers. She often seeks expensive emergency-room care because her ailments and isolation hinder her ability to make and keep scheduled appointments. She's among the 10 percent of Medicare patients who account for some 70 percent of the program's spending. Reformers argue that the system needs to be radically rebuilt to deal with such elderly patients' needs. Community-based, interdisciplinary primary care teams, for example, could provide services in the home, in clinics, and at adult day-care centers more efficiently and less wastefully than in the present facility-based system.

Several pilot programs are under way and seem effective, but creating a scalable national model is still a long way off. Any cost reductions achieved this way won't come anytime soon, and the relief will probably be modest—though service might improve significantly.

THE PROBLEMS WITH MEDICAID

Medicaid, the health-care program for low-income Americans of all ages, shares most of Medicare's problems, but with its own unique burdens. Instead of a trust fund full of empty promises, it has a black bag full of "unfunded mandates"—an accounting term that equates to "I'm taking you to dinner and sticking you with the bill."

Medicaid has grown at an alarming rate in recent years, as the recession and the loss of millions of jobs have pushed greater numbers of people into the low-income and noninsured pool. According to the Kaiser Commission on Medicaid and the Uninsured, the states paid out nearly $249 billion in calendar year 2002 for acute and other long-term care provided to nearly 40 million low-income people. Spending growth averaged nearly 12 percent in 2000 through 2002. Congress picks up half the cost, and state governments are obligated to pay the rest. To qualify for federal funds, states have to provide coverage for most people who receive federal assistance. They have the option of providing coverage to other "categorically" or "medically" needy groups under a federally mandated schedule of benefits. States receive federal matching funds for most, but not all, of the people who fall into these "needy" categories. In times of economic hardship, that budgetary hole can loom large.

In the 2001 recession, for example, states were stuck with enormous bills that produced a severe fiscal squeeze when tax receipts plummeted. The Medicaid burden reached crisis proportions and all 50 states were forced to reduce benefits, ranging from freezing payments to hospitals to limiting eligibility and increasing copayments for patients. Some states cut payments so drastically that impoverished patients have trouble finding doctors to treat them. Even so, the cutbacks at the state level only reduced the rate of growth in the Medicaid program to 9.3 percent in 2003.

Furthermore, the disaster bearing down on Medicare will only increase the strain on Medicaid. Baby boomers have already discovered that their own aged parents can qualify for Medicaid's long-term care by spending down their assets (or better, by giving away their money to fund grandchildren's college savings plans). Ominously, long-term care and other services for the elderly accounted for almost 60 percent of the growth of Medicaid spending in recent years, a sure indication that Medicaid is being swamped by an incoming tide of Medicare refugees.

THE PRESCRIPTION DRUG BENEFIT

Medicaid already includes a prescription drug benefit, and thanks to the combined legislative efforts of Republican and Democratic leaders, Medicare will pay for drugs, too, starting in 2006. But, astonishingly, this controversial promise offers *no* provision for funding! Our leaders have passed legislation that will add $534 billion in costs in the coming decade alone, with no suggestion of how to pay for it. It's as if a family already wallowing in debt went out and bought a new luxury power boat!

Let me be clear: I favor extending a helping hand to elderly people burdened with major prescription drug costs, especially low-income Americans. They carry a heavy load. About 90 percent of all senior citizens filled prescriptions in 2000, the last year for which we have total numbers, and their costs for the year averaged out to $1,500 per person. For an elderly widow living on the 2003 average Social Security payment of less than $900 a month, $1,500 is a steep price to pay. What is more, the cost has already risen at least 30 percent over the past three years. Between 2006 and 2013, when the drug benefit is being phased in, the Congressional Budget Office estimates that senior citizens will spend $1.5 trillion of their own funds for prescription drugs. Many of these people clearly need help.

Still, we cannot provide more than we can afford. By totally ignoring the question of funding, our leaders in Congress and the President have, in the name of politics, succumbed yet again to reckless and irresponsible behavior. In the words of Tom Schatz, president of Citizens Against Government Waste, "Today's politicians are raiding the paychecks of the unborn to impress senior citizens before the 2004 elections." Congress's instinct—particularly in election years—is to expand such a program rather than refine it. The politicians' lack of courage in fiscal matters is surpassed only by their aspirations. As Massachusetts Senator Ted Kennedy said when the bill passed, "This is only a down payment in our effort to fulfill our responsibility to seniors."

CONGRESS STUMBLES IN THE DARK

Our congressional leaders might have acted more responsibly if they'd known what they were doing, although history provides little evidence to support such an assumption. In fact, Congress was hoodwinked by the Bush Administration's unscrupulous effort to conceal the true costs of the prescription drug program. Our lawmakers passed the bill on the premise that the cost would be $400 billion in its first 10 years, with major outlays deferred until 2006, and phasing in gradually thereafter until fully effective in 2013. With that assurance, the bill squeaked through a bitterly divided Congress.

Only later did the Bush Administration admit that the first decade's cost would be $534 billion, not $400 billion, and that Medicare's chief actuary, Richard S. Foster, had been ordered by his superior not to divulge his figures to Congress. Furthermore, because the benefit is being gradually phased in, costs for the *second* decade will be vastly higher at around $1 trillion. In other words, at a minimum the bill will add a total of around $1.5 trillion to Medicare's unfunded liabilities over the next 20 years.

The plan's cost beyond that is problematical because medical price inflation is such a question mark. Most projections use a highly optimistic assumption, mentioned earlier, that medical costs will rise only 1 percent faster than the general cost of living, rather than the 3 percent we've experienced in recent years. Drug costs are increasing even faster, rising three percentage points more than health-care costs in general. Even using the best-case scenario, the added drug benefit will raise the cost of Medicare to 24 percent of all income-tax revenues in 2026 and 40 percent in 2043. By 2043, unfunded Social Security costs will also equal 40 percent of income taxes. That leaves just 20 percent of tax receipts to pay for everything else in the federal budget, from defense to roads and bridges to education to research to homeland security.

These numbers are impossible to sustain. One way or another, this trend has to be brought to an end before entitlement spending eats the bulk of any tax revenues. The longer we delay acting, the more catastrophic it will be for our children and grandchildren.

THE CHOICES ARE STARK

There are only four choices available to our leaders: We can raise taxes, reduce benefits, change eligibility guidelines, or continue borrowing to finance Medicare and Medicaid. Choosing to do the job through increased taxes alone would add $1,168 to each household's tax burden in 2010, a figure that would climb to $4,000 in 2030—a move that would surely trigger a tax rebellion. When Alan Greenspan had the temerity to suggest cutting benefits, he touched off a political firestorm; people seem to believe that any adjustment at all in current benefits or eligibility would mean that the government is reneging on what amounts to a sacred promise. But the fourth option, continued borrowing, is equally untenable. It would further increase our already dangerously high national debt. This, in turn, would push up interest rates and raise our debt service to a crippling level. The economy would be plunged into recession, or worse.

The best course of action for the Medicare shortfall may be some combination of increased taxes and reduced benefits or eligibility adjustments. But our leaders—Democrats and Republicans—must act now to find the least painful way to cut back. We might, for instance, raise the retirement age and postpone the start of Medicare coverage. Or we could increase copayments for beneficiaries. Or we could limit benefits according to recipients' incomes or accumulated assets.

One important precedent for reducing entitlement costs by just this kind of means testing went almost unnoticed in last year's Medicare bill, overshadowed by the prescription-drug controversy. Until now, Social Security and Medicare have been need-blind in the distribution of benefits, entitling millionaires and paupers alike to the same schedule of payments. Under the little-noticed provision, premiums for Medicare Part B will soon be tied to income. Starting in 2007, instead of a uniform monthly premium that pays one-fourth of the Part B expenditures, seniors with annual incomes above $80,000 ($160,000 for couples) will pay a premium designed to cover up to 80 percent of the costs. Higher-income seniors are likely to lobby fiercely to repeal this provision before it kicks in. But if it survives, it could provide a much-needed road map for efforts to hold down entitlement costs while still providing benefits to those who need them most.

There is no easy solution to the dilemma of Medicare and Medicaid. All the choices are painful. But our leaders must find a solution. And it is our job to insist that they do so. A humane and just society cannot leave the elderly, the sick, and the indigent to die in the gutter. But neither can it risk bringing down the U.S. economy, or bequeathing an unbearable burden of debt to our children and grandchildren.

QUIETING THE CRITICS

Without immediate action, the United States is edging closer to the abyss of an almost unimaginable financial disaster. Whether by design, irrational optimism, stupidity, or lack of political courage, our elected representatives have blithely ignored the financial ruin that lies ahead. Some, determined to strangle "big government," deny that such a catastrophe could ever befall us. Are we not the greatest nation on earth?

I have yet to hear anyone successfully defend our disastrous debt-and-deficit spiral. There just aren't any arguments that hold up under careful scrutiny.

In the next chapter, I will present some of the criticisms that have been leveled against the charges I have made. You may have heard some of them yourself. But as I rebut these unsound arguments one by one, I believe you will be more convinced than ever that we have no time to lose if we hope to save our great country.

CHAPTER 9

ANTICIPATING THE CRITICS

THE IDEA OF financial failure is hard to fathom for America. We are a rich, militarily strong superpower that, for decades, has basked in the world's admiration and respect. The world's common language is English; up to now, the international currency has been the dollar. Can we truly be in danger of becoming a second-rate economic power?

Our political leaders in the Administration and in Congress tend to be optimists who talk enthusiastically of rosy scenarios under their stewardship. Why? Because many of the voters only want to hear good news. They are involved in a mutual dance of denial. Even the crop of Democrats running for election this year—John Kerry, for the presidency; the hundreds of representatives, senators, and challengers—haven't painted a canvas as black as what I foresee.

Could I be wrong, and could all of them be right? I'll tell you why I'm not wrong by rebutting the major arguments my critics are sure to make one by one.

- *The optimists say:* Our current political leaders—the Bush Administration and members of the Senate and House of Representatives—aren't to blame for today's deficits and the way they are escalating the national debt. The current river of red ink simply reflects recent shocks beyond anyone's control, from the bursting of the stock-market bubble in 2000 and the war on terror in the wake of 9/11 to the 2001 economic recession and a wave of corporate scandals.

Arguably, all those factors played a part in piling up the budget deficits of the past three years. But at most, according to the nonpartisan Congressional Budget Office (CBO), reduced revenues from slow economic growth accounted for only a third of the 2002 federal budget deficit. They accounted for a fifth of 2003's. Moreover, these events are behind us now, except for our ongoing homeland security initiatives and the costs of our occupation of Afghanistan and Iraq (and the Administration has, astonishingly, omitted many of those costs from its "official" deficit reckoning for 2004). For now, at least, the stock market has been rebounding (it was up 25 percent last year); the corporate miscreants are being prosecuted; and the economy is growing. Yet our present and future deficits continue to spiral upward, overwhelming revenues. And one of President Bush's top priorities is to make permanent the major tax cuts he enacted in past years, without suggesting where the necessary revenues to replace that money will come from.

As an excuse for our record-breaking deficits, the reasons given are increasingly suspect. In fact, the CBO recently estimated that the economy's weakness would explain only 6 percent of the country's projected 2004 deficit, which the congressional watchdog puts at $477 billion (the Administration projects a deficit of $521 billion)—again, not including war spending that will add another $50 billion at least.

The numbers confirm that the current massive deficits are not the result of unforeseen economic shocks but are built into the budget. Made inevitable by ever-expanding spending—domestic spending, not including defense, is up 27 percent since Bush took office—and a deepening reduction in revenues from President Bush's tax cuts, which he wants to make permanent, the huge deficits will continue for the foreseeable future. The sharpest losses of revenue won't hit the Treasury until 2006. Princeton economist Paul Krugman puts the loss of revenue over the next decade at an astonishing *$800 billion* if the President succeeds in making the cuts permanent. Yet no offsetting spending cuts have been proposed.

There's no rational way to blame the coming disaster on the events and the economic shocks of years past. The blame goes to the Bush Administration and our Congress—our elected officials, and their appointees—and to the fiscal policies they set and the budgets and tax cuts they have legislated and signed.

- *The optimists say:* The interest we pay on the national debt isn't a major budget expense. It's not a real burden on the economy. We can easily afford a few pennies on the dollar.

Obviously, these Pollyannas haven't bothered to look at the undeniable cost of interest on our national debt. Again, interest on the debt came to $318 billion in 2003, when interest rates were the lowest in 46 years. It's the largest item in the budget after health and human services and military spending. It works out to nearly $1 billion a day, or more than $1,000 a year for every man, woman, and child in the United States. Debt service ate up 17 percent of all tax revenues in 2003, a monstrous drain on our government before we could even begin spending on what the country needed. And as our debt increases—it has risen by $1.5 trillion under George W. Bush since the end of 2001—and interest rates go up, our debt-service payments could skyocket.

If we had had that $318 billion in our pockets to spend on current requirements, it would have bought a long list of things, from benefits for the brave men and women who have served in our military forces to improvements in education for our children and help for the unemployed. Or it could have paid for our space program and for better homeland protection against terrorist threats. So numbed are we by the stratospheric numbers casually tossed about by our politicians that we sometimes lose sight of the fact that we're talking about truckloads of real money that could be used to solve critical problems.

Do billions of dollars of interest costs sound like "a few cents on the dollar" that we can easily afford? In the real world, where I hang my hat, there is nothing either tolerable or affordable about government policies that squander hundreds of billions of our hard-earned dollars merely to sustain the reckless spending habits of our elected representatives. You and I cannot run our lives that way. Neither can the federal government.

- *The optimists say:* We owe the national debt to ourselves, so it doesn't hurt us. The money stays in our economy. Investors who buy Treasuries get interest payments, and they either spend the money, which speeds up the economy, or invest it, which provides growth.

This argument dates back to Abba Lerner, a Russian-born disciple of John Maynard Keynes and one of the leading lights of Keynesian economics in the 1930s. It's one of the basic rationalizations for budget deficits. And it's true—as far as it goes.

One problem these days, however, is that America's citizens aren't saving enough to finance our annual deficits or to refinance our national debt (as I noted in Chapter 6, our savings rate is at an all-time low of between 1 percent and 2 percent of income). So our Treasury's bonds and notes that are put up for sale are increasingly being bought by foreign investors and foreign governments. As recently as 1992, foreigners owned just 18 percent of our publicly held national debt; they now hold approximately *40 percent*. That means the interest we pay with money generated here is being sent abroad into foreign hands, helping to foster foreign economies to the tune of more than $100 billion a year.

Should we be worried?

Yes. Again, even if our friends abroad lend back to us every dollar they earn on our debt, that only means we are running up still more debt, and paying still more interest each year to people who don't live here and who don't necessarily share our goals, interests, and beliefs. It's not far-fetched to imagine us one day held captive by global financial markets—or, worse yet, at the mercy of hostile foreign governments. If foreign investors, who send us more than $40 billion every month, start worrying that we are not going to repay them, they are sure to demand higher interest. As a result, the interest burden of carrying our debt would rise astronomically. This situation is analogous to betting the deed to your house in a high-stakes poker game. If the cards fall the wrong way, you and your family are at the mercy of the fellow holding the winning hand. And our situation gets more worrisome, and less tolerable, with every note or bond that winds up in foreign accounts.

- *The optimists say:* Being in hock to foreigners won't affect our international standing. After all, the United States was built with money from Europe. The critical factor nowadays is that we lead the world, and no one can question our dominance in foreign policy and military might, no matter how much we owe.

In the aftermath of World War II, our reach and influence grew steadily along with our wealth. With the fall of the Soviet Union, we became the world's undisputed superpower. But that is already changing. In world councils these days, we are beginning to feel a chill directed toward the chronic debtor. You can't continue to run the world from a weakening economic position.

It's no secret that the rest of the world has long had a love-hate relationship with the United States—envious of our wealth and freedom, and yet resentful of our strong-arm tactics in world forums. Now, in the wake of our preemptive invasion of Iraq in the spring of 2003, foreign anger and discontent have intensified.

Surveys conducted by the Pew Research Center find enormous skepticism about our motives in invading Iraq. Large majorities in France and Germany—traditionally our strong allies—believe the United States seeks "to control Mideast oil and dominate the world." It is a view that is shared by predominantly Muslim countries. And longtime friends in countries as diverse as Brazil, South Korea, Turkey, and Indonesia have grown increasingly distrustful of us.

Sooner or later, our Asian, European, and Middle Eastern creditors are likely to remind us just who's controlling the purse strings, either by refusing to lend more money because of greater perceived risk, or by threatening to choke off the flow of cash unless we back off a foreign-policy maneuver with which they disagree.

- *The optimists say:* Future generations will not be burdened by the current national debt. In fact, they will benefit from the investments we make with the money we are borrowing.

That might be true—if we were actually borrowing to make investments like repairing and expanding the nation's decaying infrastructure. You can justify taking out a loan to finance the renovation or repair of a real asset such as a house or a business, or to fuel growth by adding more stores or capacity or buying a larger combine to speed up grain harvesting. It's even legitimate for a nation to run a wartime deficit, because the safety and security of those who will have to repay the debt hangs in the balance. To the extent that our deficit is paying for subduing terrorism and rebuilding Afghanistan and Iraq—$87 billion in 2003—it could be considered a legitimate investment in our future. But the other three quarters of last year's deficit spending mostly went to pay the government's daily bills and to finance lots of legislative pork, not for any real investment purpose.

What is worse, we are even spending the money we pretend to be saving for future needs. As I discussed earlier, the surpluses that are supposed to be piling up in trust funds for use in later years have been absconded with to pay for current deficit spending. Nor do these so-called loans count as part of the official deficit, even though they do get added into the national debt, which future generations will be required to pay. In 2003, the government "borrowed" $161 billion from the trust funds. Add that figure to the $375 billion of officially acknowledged red ink in fiscal 2003 and the real deficit would have been $536 billion. The deficit forecasted for 2004 by the President—$521 billion—would soar to $675 billion if trust fund borrowings were added in. This is money our children and grandchildren will have to pay back. And the interest payments on the escalating national debt will be staggering. Remember, President Bush has promised that "we will not deny, we will not ignore, and we will not pass along our problems to other Congresses, to other presidents and other generations." But his actions completely belie his words. What we have is a legacy of runaway spending and irresponsible tax cuts.

- *The optimists say:* It's okay to borrow from the trust funds to finance the deficit, because it eases pressure on the money markets and helps keep interest rates low.

This is a real can of worms. As long as the trust funds run surpluses, the government has to do something with the money—it can't just stack up dollar bills in some gigantic strongbox. Because the safest investment in the world has long been U.S. Treasury bonds, Congress decreed that trust-fund surpluses should be salted away in the form of government bonds and notes. What that means, of course, is that the Treasury is borrowing the money from future retirees, replacing the trust funds' real assets with nothing more than IOUs from the government. Undoubtedly, this arrangement does help to hold down interest rates, because the government isn't forced to flood the markets with debt offerings, which would drive up rates. And low interest rates do benefit the economy up to a certain point. The drawback is that very low interest rates discourage American households from saving. This, in turn, means that more and more of our deficit has to be financed by foreign lenders.

As for the hole in the trust funds, when it comes time to pay for the retirement of the huge baby-boom generation (the first wave will start collecting benefits in 2008), the government will be forced to return to the bond markets with *massive* offerings. It will have to borrow to replace the funds it siphoned off in past years, because that sum will be needed to pay the retiring boomers' benefits. And it will have to borrow again to pay for current expenses that it used to borrow from trust-fund surpluses. Inevitably, that will increase the pressure on the bond markets, and rates will rise. So the benefit of borrowing from the trust funds is, at best, fleeting. And over the long haul, it's likely to be catastrophic.

Honest accounting would openly reflect the borrowing from the trust fund so that we the voters could see the truth behind the promises of benefits without costs. As long as the surpluses exist, we must account for them separately and include any borrowing from them in the official reckoning of the annual budget deficit. That was once the law. But Congress changed it, adopting the so-called unified budget that allows the government to conceal the true depth of its recklessness. Honest accounting won't fix the mess we're in. But American citizens, who ultimately bear the burden, surely deserve to know just how bad things are. They need to be able to determine which politicians are telling the truth and which are not.

- *The optimists say:* Low taxes are better for the economy than low deficits. Paying less money in taxes leaves people with more money to spend. The deficit is good because it keeps taxes low, stimulates spending, and creates jobs.

It's true that when the economy is sluggish, the government can give it a push by keeping taxes low, running a deficit, and letting the Federal Reserve pump additional money into circulation, stimulating spending and creating demand that encourages businesses to hire more workers. But if the economy is already accelerating, that same low-tax, deficit-running, easy-money scenario is a recipe for inflation. And inflation inevitably pushes up interest rates as well as prices. In the long run, it slows the economy.

Do we run the risk of a recession if we cut spending or raise taxes? Yes. But a brief slowdown to reduce the deficit would set the stage for a long, steady boom. My view is borne out by what happened in the 1990s. With the federal budget deep in red ink, the first President Bush courageously raised taxes. Bill Clinton followed suit. During

Clinton's first term, both the deficit and unemployment began to decline while the economy started to grow. Within a few short years, the deficits had turned to surpluses, unemployment was at multi-decade lows, and the economy was booming.

In the long run, higher deficits act as a drag on the economy. Why? Continuing high deficits persuade investors to demand higher interest rates. And it's the long term, not the short term, that we should be concerned about, because we live and do business over the long haul. Our present policy of cutting taxes while rapidly increasing spending is a superhighway to national bankruptcy. If we continue to rely on government borrowing, the inevitable result will be not just more debt owed to foreigners, but a reduction in America's capital stock of goods that are used to produce other goods and services. Rather than lending back our interest payments, foreign investors will use the dollars to buy more real estate, shares of U.S. companies, and whole companies themselves.

If we are to restore America's credibility and credit rating in the global markets, and if we are to secure an economic future for our children and grandchildren, we have to demonstrate fiscal responsibility—we have to start reducing our deficits.

- *The optimists say:* The deficit and the national debt may sound scary, but you've got to look at them in perspective. Our economy is large enough to be able to afford big annual deficits and a huge national debt.

The truth of this statement depends on just how big big is. In 2004, our deficit will equal an estimated 4.5 percent of the gross domestic product (GDP), the dollar amount of all the goods and services this country produces, and that's not counting the trust-fund money we borrow to make the deficit look smaller, or the cost of our continuing occupation in Iraq. If we count the money borrowed from the trust funds, the 2004 budget deficit as a percentage of GDP exceeds the post–World War II record level of 6 percent set in 1983.

(There was no surplus in the trust funds in 1983, so to make an accurate comparison we need to add the money borrowed from the trust fund to the current annual deficit.) Adding in those borrowings widens this year's deficit to about 6.5 percent of GDP.

Can our economy carry such a load? Not if the economic experts know what they're talking about. Most economists agree that 5 percent of GDP is the point at which a deficit becomes an intolerable burden for an economy to carry. The European Union limits its members' deficits to 3 percent of GDP. Germany and France are now facing the threat of discipline for exceeding the limit. Unfortunately, there's no one to discipline the United States—until the markets turn against us.

As for the national debt, it's now $7.3 trillion and rising fast. Measured as a percentage of GDP, the debt soared to more than 60 percent at the beginning of this year, compared to only 34 percent in 1980. Economists generally agree that any debt over 60 percent of GDP is too great a burden to carry.

• *The optimists say:* Financing the debt will never be a problem. Investors love our Treasury bonds and notes; they have been the world's standard of value for almost 50 years now. After all, where else can people invest and feel absolutely secure?

I hate to burst the optimists' bubble, but financing the debt is already a problem. As I mentioned earlier, Americans depend on help from abroad to finance the national debt. But Treasury notes and bonds and the dollar itself are increasingly risky assets, given our low interest rates and the falling value of the dollar against foreign currencies. Euros are looking pretty enticing these days. Remember, in the past two years, the dollar has lost nearly a third of its value against the euro. It is trading at an all-time low. Foreign investors are increasingly alarmed by our lack of a credible budget policy. Treasury bonds have held their value only because the Chinese and Japanese governments have been huge buyers. At the beginning of 2004, Japan held $577 billion of our government bonds; China held $148 billion. These countries invest in these bonds for reasons that have nothing to do with our credit standing, but rather reflect their own perceived national interests. And those interests could change overnight.

We may still be the world's largest financial market, but we are far from the only one. And you can bet that foreign investors are eyeing the alternatives as our reckless fiscal behavior goes unchecked. Counting private and public debt, we need our foreigners to lend us more than $40 billion a *month* to keep our spending binge going. Not surprisingly, these investors are beginning to wonder how we can ever repay all they are owed. Foreign holdings of our government bonds total $1.5 trillion. Foreign investors have cut back significantly on the flow of loans in the past year or so, preferring to buy our assets outright rather than lend us more money. This is not a favorable trend.

Unless we put our fiscal house in order, we are in danger of losing our long-standing, gold-plated reputation in the global investment community.

- *The optimists say:* It's a myth that budget deficits cause inflation. Inflation in the United States was highest back in the 1980s, when deficits were less than half today's level. Now, when deficits are high and rising, inflation has been running at only about 2 percent a year.

To the critics who point to recent low inflation rates as evidence that deficits have no bearing on prices, I would remind them that there is always a lag between cause and effect. The inflation of the 1980s can be traced back to deficits run up in the 1960s and 1970s. The fact is that our current excesses just haven't caught up with us yet. This lag is a major reason why politicians can pretend their promises have unrealistically low costs.

Throughout history, no nation has consistently been able to live beyond its means without spawning an inflationary cycle. The mechanism is always the same: At first, the government finances its deficit by selling bonds to investors at home and abroad. As the deficits and the total debt grow, the investors demand higher returns to offset the added risk of default. Eventually, they grow reluctant to lend at all, even at higher rates. So the government "monetizes" the debt, which means that, instead of borrowing what it needs, it simply prints more money. (Brazil and Argentina provide two recent examples.) Suddenly, there is too much money in the economy chasing too few goods, and inflation begins to spiral out of control.

Inflation is already beginning to heat up in the United States. Many economic observers fear this is the beginning of a new and devastating cycle. Just because inflation appears to be in check at the moment doesn't mean our deficits will not trigger the terrifying specter of rapidly rising inflation.

- *The optimists say:* We can grow our way out of our problems. Economic growth will provide much bigger tax revenues, even at reduced tax rates. Plenty of money will be available for future obligations as the recovery continues.

Nonsense. Two-thirds of the national budget already goes for mandatory items—debt interest and entitlement spending—and these two categories are growing faster than any conceivable rise in revenues from economic growth.

I've already gone over the inevitable course of debt service. Annual deficits will add inexorably to the total debt, and rising interest rates will multiply the cost of carrying it. And in just four years, the 77 million baby boomers will begin to retire. When they do, they will be getting not just Social Security benefits but Medicare and Medicaid, too—and thanks to Congress's generosity, a $534 billion Medicare benefit for prescription drugs. There is *no money* put away to pay for *any* of this; all the trust-fund money has been spent. So we will have to raise the ever-rising tide of funds as we go.

Economic growth could, in fact, make the problem worse. A growing economy means growth in wages and medical costs, which would add to the total Social Security and Medicare benefits retirees could claim.

- *The optimists say:* Our deficits are our own business. America is sick and tired of being lectured about them. Foreign investors, their governments, and international institutions should shut up and mind their own business.

This is more a gripe than an argument against the dangers of our budget deficits. But it deserves a comment nonetheless. We are indeed being lectured, and it's insulting. Both the World Bank and the International Monetary Fund have warned the United States that its record twin deficits—trade and budget—pose a threat to global economic stability. That kind of talk is usually reserved for Third World economies—banana republics, if you will.

But rather than be insulted, we should be *ashamed.* The way we conduct our fiscal affairs is, in fact, the world's business. If the biggest economy in the world suffers the kind of meltdown I've been talking about, it will spread hardship and pain around the globe. No country and no person will be insulated. There will be no sure way for anyone to escape, either by investing in gold or some other supposed safe haven. Remember, history teaches us that in countries where the economy collapses, political stability and personal safety have always been at risk. If anyone comes out unscathed, it will be a lucky accident. So everyone in the world has an interest in what we do—and a right to talk about it.

- *The optimists say:* The deficit is only temporary. President Bush has promised to cut it in half in five years. We should trust that the President and Congress will do what's needed to solve our problems.

If only I could believe that 40 years of irresponsible behavior would suddenly come to an end. But actions speak louder than words. Experience tells me that political expediency usually trumps good judgment. Buy now and pay later has been transformed by our politicians into receive now and let the next generation pay later. The next election is never far from a politician's mind. Presidential candidates and other politicians can win popularity by cutting taxes and spending money on things that the public wants, even if we can't afford them.

At various times over the years, our politicians have come up with gimmicks designed to keep deficits under control. In 1940, Congress passed, and President Roosevelt signed, a statutory limit on the national debt of $49 billion. Unfortunately, the limit turned out to be like the ceiling on an elevator—movable.

Every time government bumps up against it, Congress and the President push a button and raise it another floor or two. The limit is now set at $7.384 trillion. It will need to be raised again this year, and you can be sure it will be.

Far more effective deficit control occurred when Congress, in 1990, passed what was called the "Pay-Go law." It required that any tax cuts or spending boosts be matched by equivalent tax increases or benefit reductions. It's no accident that the deficits started shrinking and actually turned into surpluses when Pay-Go was in effect. But when the law expired in 2001, those in Congress who were hoping to get reelected by bringing home extra bacon quickly killed a bid to extend it. As I write, fiscal conservatives in both parties are making a bid to revive it. But Republican House leaders are pushing to apply Pay-Go only to spending increases, which means President Bush's tax cuts wouldn't have to be offset with cuts elsewhere in the budget.

I'm not betting on success in any form. Up to now, no politician wanting to be reelected could tell voters they have to face serious pain to correct our fiscal follies, especially when opposing candidates were promising pain avoidance. This has to change *now*.

In February 2002, well after the stock-market crash, the terrorist attacks, and the recession, the Administration's numbers crunchers projected that the budget would be only $14 billion in the red in fiscal 2004 and would actually return to surplus the following year. As we now know, the real deficit is $521 billion for 2004 and rising. And as for the Bush Administration's claim that the deficit will be cut in half in five years, a bipartisan group of budget analysts has arrived at a far different conclusion. Taking into account probable future costs based on current budget policies—the tax cuts, the Medicare drug benefit, extra defense spending to fight the war on terrorism, growth in benefit programs to keep pace with inflation and an expanding population—this group sees annual deficits of $400 billion, $500 billion, even $600 billion far into the future.

Whether by design or delusion, the promises our government has made have not been kept. They have proved to be little more than empty reassurances. The problems facing us are real. And they are urgent. We can no longer risk our future in hopes that someone else will finally make good on those promises. We must acknowledge the extreme seriousness of our situation so that we can work together to solve it before it is too late. No one can tell for sure just how much time we have to come up with solutions. The inevitable economic calamities may be held off for years. On the other hand, some unforeseen event could trigger a crisis at any moment. The sooner we act, the better.

What should we do?

The second part of this book contains my prescription for averting disaster. In the chapter that follows, I will first look at some neighboring countries that have suffered similar fiscal calamities. There is no better teacher than experience, particularly when we can learn our lessons by studying the failures (and successes) of others. In terms of economic calamities, learning from the bleachers is far preferable to firsthand personal experience.

PART TWO

AVERTING DISASTER

*Many nations have sped
headlong toward financial ruin.
A few have come to their senses in time
to avoid disaster. Our courage
and political will must guide
us in changing course and averting disaster.*

CHAPTER 10

LEARNING FROM THE EXPERIENCE OF OTHERS

"THOSE WHO CANNOT remember the past are condemned to repeat it," philosopher George Santayana famously observed. It's a sad fact of life that every nation that continually spends beyond its means sooner or later pays the price for its recklessness. Civilization is littered with governments that have collapsed due to irresponsible economic policies. Indeed, a crash like the one we are heading for has followed runaway national debt and deficits in many governments throughout history. If our leaders continue down the road to ruin we have been traversing for the past four decades, it will be because they willfully closed their eyes to the lessons of history. And if we let them do it, we will deserve what we get.

Nine years ago, Canada faced a plight similar to ours. But by reversing course, it narrowly averted collapse.

THE FLIGHT OF THE LOONIE

In January 1995, Canada seemed to be rushing headlong toward economic calamity. Its budget deficit had skyrocketed by 50 percent in five years, reaching $42 billion (Canadian dollars), or 6 percent of its gross domestic product (our own estimated 2004 deficit stands at 4.5

percent of our GDP). Its national debt totaled a towering 70 percent of GDP (ours now stands at 62 percent), and Canada depended on foreign investors to finance the lion's share of it. The Canadian dollar, amiably known as "the Loonie" for the bird depicted on its coin, was sinking fast against the world's currencies.

Then *The Wall Street Journal* weighed in with a dose of shock therapy that jolted the country down to its permafrost. A caustic editorial headlined "Bankrupt Canada?" started off: "Check out Canada, which has now become an honorary member of the Third World in the unmanageability of its debt problem." The editorial went on to warn that Canada was such a basket case it might have to "call in the [International Monetary Fund] to stabilize its falling currency."

Finance Minister Paul Martin, whose first budget was criticized as woefully indulgent, had assured the IMF that cutting spending was his first priority. But the biting editorial galvanized the government into action. With even liberal politicians grasping the danger, the public seemed ready to swallow a dose of fiscal discipline. Austerity budgets in the provinces of Alberta and Saskatchewan met with surprisingly little opposition.

Taking their cue, Martin and Prime Minister Jean Chrétien attacked the federal budget with a meat ax, cutting nearly every program in sight. "We knew that nothing less than a fundamental rethinking of government was necessary," Chrétien said later, "not just to clean up the fiscal mess, but to ensure that the Government of Canada never again found itself in such a position." They went through every department and every program, asking three basic questions: (1) Does it make sense for government to be doing this at all? (2) If so, should it be a national responsibility, or one better addressed at the provincial or municipal level? (3) If we continue to address the problem at the national level, how can we do it more efficiently?

Chrétien and Martin reduced aid for industry. They cut such formerly untouchable services as the spousal-abuse centers. They slashed foreign aid by 21 percent. They even pared back the military roster by 14 percent. Some programs lost 60 percent of their spending budgets from one year to the next. Federal employment plunged by 45,000, or 14 percent of the total, with some departments cut in half. (If we were to cut 14 percent of the federal government, federal employment would drop by 266,000.) Only weeks after the *Journal's* editorial, Martin unveiled his austerity budget. It received a warm reception not just from bankers but from opinion shapers across the board. Chrétien and Martin, who sold their program in a series of public hearings across the nation, won over all but a few die-hard activists from organized labor.

Most important, the old-time religion worked its healing miracle. Steadily shrinking deficits turned, in fiscal 1998, into what has proved to be a continuing string of surpluses—a feat unmatched by any country among the prestigious Group of Eight major industrialized democracies. Martin vowed to use half of the surpluses for social spending and the other half for tax cuts and debt reduction; Chrétien pledged to cut the national debt to 60 percent of GDP by 2000. (Chrétien kept his promise.)

John Manley, who succeeded Martin as finance minister in 2002, could boast that, far from being a Third World country, Canada had become "a Northern Tiger economy." *Business Week* magazine updated *The Wall Street Journal* editorial, labeling Canada the "Maple Leaf Miracle." In 2003, a grateful nation elected Martin prime minister. As for the Loonie, the old bird is flying again: Canada's dollar has risen from its low point of 62 U.S. cents to 76 cents as of the spring of 2004.

WHAT AWAITS US IF WE FAIL

Argentina was one of the world's major economic powers in the early twentieth century. With vast tracts of rich soil for growing crops and a wealth of natural resources, it was once the fifth most productive nation in the world. No longer. In the bitter words of an Argentine national joke, "Only the Argentines could screw up a country as blessed as this one."

Tracing its downfall takes us through decades of military misrule, economic turmoil, and defeat by Britain in the 1982 war over the Falkland Islands, following which Argentina was returned to civilian rule under the democratically elected government of Raúl Alfonsín. Commendably, Alfonsín focused on ending human rights abuses. Unfortunately, he coupled his crusade with massive spending on social reforms when there was no money to pay for them. In 1985, the national deficit reached *11 percent* of the country's gross domestic product. When a nation's deficit grows as large as Argentina's, government borrowing soaks up all the savings the economy can generate. When there is nothing left to pay the bills, the country must either borrow from foreigners or print more money. In the case of Argentina, after foreign investors proved reluctant to lend, the government revved up the printing presses to meet its obligations. The subsequent flood of pesos triggered an annual inflation rate of 672 percent.

By 1990, Argentina had fallen to 70th place in the ranks of productive nations. Its per-capita GDP actually shrank by 20 percent between 1983 and 1990, with a total production per person of only $2,560. The government made scant effort to cut Argentina's bloated bureaucracy and chronic crony capitalism. Corruption was endemic, and taxes were so high that they were uncollectible. The country's foreign debt of $55.2 billion had grown to 70 percent of GDP, and Argentina's repayment record was so poor that investors collected only 19 cents of every dollar they held in Argentine debt. The exchange rate ballooned from two pesos to the U.S. dollar in 1987 to 9,900 to the dollar in 1990.

Inflation averaged a devastating 1,350 percent in 1990. It was so dire that items purchased in the afternoon cost more than they had in the morning. In an effort to restore some semblance of value to its money, the country chopped six zeros off the currency in three years, thereby shrinking a 10-million-peso note to just 10 pesos. By 1990, the people were rioting and begging for change.

In 1991, President Carlos Menem imposed a dose of economic discipline for a time by cracking down on tax evaders, downsizing the bureaucracy, cutting subsidies, proposing a balanced budget, and opening up trade. Moreover, he prohibited the government from printing money to finance its deficits. When his reforms failed to stabilize the economy, Menem decided to peg the peso exchange rate one-to-one with the U.S. dollar. This boosted investor confidence and helped rein in inflation.

The results were spectacular for a while: The budget deficit, which was running at 6 percent of GDP in 1990, fell to less than 3 percent of GDP in 1991, then slid below 2 percent in 1992. The economy produced real, inflation-adjusted growth of 5 percent in 1991 and 6 percent in 1992. It was dramatic evidence of what can happen when a country gets serious about tackling its deficit problems. The economic rebalancing was not without pain, of course—notably, rising unemployment and a recession—but most voters were willing to bite the bullet in the belief that the rewards would be long term.

The sticking point proved to be the peso peg. By adopting a currency exchange rate that was disconnected from its own economy, Argentina had essentially relinquished control over its monetary policy. The country's lenders were reassured, but Argentina couldn't find a way to undo the peg when it proved troublesome. During the 1997 Asian currency crisis, for example, circumstances dictated a rate adjustment, but Argentina was unable to respond.

Neighboring Brazil devalued its currency by 28 percent, effectively undercutting the prices of many of Argentina's exports. Argentina managed to keep its exports rising by slashing their prices an average of 18 percent, but bringing in the cash needed to repay its dollar-denominated debts became ever more difficult. Eventually, the budget fell back into deficit, and the attempt at fiscal austerity failed.

In December 2001, the International Monetary Fund forced Argentina into default by refusing to hand over a $1.24 billion loan payment promised as part of an earlier $21.6 billion rescue package. In January 2002, with the economy in free fall and the financial system paralyzed, the National Congress installed the populist regime of Eduardo Duhalde—the fifth president to take office in two weeks. Duhalde unpegged the peso and devalued the currency. But he was still unable to halt the economic collapse. Joblessness ran over 20 percent, and the people rose up in work stoppages and demonstrations that turned to riots after the government put tight restrictions on bank withdrawals. With GDP off by 21 percent since 1998, the value of the peso down by 70 percent, and unemployment spiking to 22 percent of the labor force, Argentina defaulted yet again in November 2002.

In May of 2003, an obscure provincial governor, Nestor Kirchner, was inaugurated as president, pledging, in time-honored fashion, to fight corruption, reform the courts, and end human rights abuses. With nearly half the population mired in poverty, crime on the rise, and an economy still in crisis, his task would be difficult. Nonetheless, by the spring of 2004, the currency devaluation had cut costs for manufacturers, and the IMF was forecasting 5.5 percent growth in Argentina's economy for the year.

Whether or not Argentina is finally on the road to recovery is still an open question. What is not open to question is that out-of-control government spending produced massive deficits that led to unsustainable foreign borrowing, runaway inflation, crushing unemployment, and years of untold hardship.

I can't help but think that memories of their glorious past in the early part of the century lulled Argentineans into thinking, "It can never happen here." Could the United States be brought down by the same complacency? Argentina's 2001 crisis occurred when its deficit, measured as a share of its GDP, was smaller than what the United States is running today. But with its reputation shattered, creditors were in no mood to cut it any slack.

With each passing year and every drop of red ink, America's own fiscal credibility loses some of its luster. As I noted earlier, both the World Bank and the IMF have warned us that our trade and budget deficits are a danger to global economic stability. Temporary deficits will be overlooked by the markets if a borrower has a history of sound finance. But if we consistently fail to balance the books, particularly when that imbalance is the result of budget-busting policies that we actively pursue, such as tax cuts in the face of out-of-control spending and wholly improbable projections for expenditures and revenues going forward, the markets may quit giving us the benefit of the doubt. Never before in U.S. history has an American president attempted to cut taxes while waging a war. In fact, America's wartime presidents have increased taxes to help cover the costs.

As I pointed out in Chapter 6, if foreign investors were to lose faith in our ability to make payments on our debt, interest rates would surely soar, and the value of the dollar would plummet. If we continue to act like a banana republic, eventually we can expect the markets to treat us like one.

A WASTE OF RICHES

Argentina's neighbor Brazil is another sad tale of squandered potential. With the world's ninth-largest economy (GDP is equivalent to $447 billion) and fifth-biggest population (178 million), Brazil could be a huge economic power—if only it could brake its unchecked spending.

Brazil boasts a sophisticated manufacturing industry and is a leading arms and small-aircraft producer. It trails only the United States in food exports, and last year, largely as a result of its booming agricultural sector, the country posted a record trade surplus equivalent to nearly $25 billion.

Yet fiscal instability and rampant inflation have kept the South American giant from being a star on the world stage. The rate of inflation has, at times, been stupefying: A price index set at 100 in March 1986 reached 3,041,400 by February 1991, when it was discontinued. Like neighboring Argentina, Brazil hacked six zeros off its currency between 1989 and 1992. Its total debt, both foreign and domestic, is the developing world's largest at about $256 billion, and investors have long shunned its notes—with good reason: Brazil often delayed repayment in the past and completely suspended all debt repayments in 1989.

Politically and economically, Brazil has been on a long roller-coaster ride. In the 1960s, growing at double-digit rates, it was known as the "miracle economy." But in the next decade, inflation began to heat up as double-digit price rises boiled into triple-digit blowouts. Meanwhile, foreign borrowing exploded, and foreign investment shrank. By the end of the 1980s, GDP growth had slowed to the low single digits, leaving Brazil with a glut of unpayable foreign debt, widespread corruption, and out-of-control spending.

In the 1990s, despite a recession and galloping inflation, the legislature kept right on spending, financing the government deficits by running the printing press. Soon prices were rising at about 20 percent monthly.

Brazil's first socialist president in 40 years, Luis Inacio Lula da Silva—or "Lula," as he is popularly known—took office in 2002 after promising to end hunger, tackle the ever-present corruption, improve education, create jobs, and spur annual economic growth of 5 percent a year. The financial world braced for still more spending and still faster inflation. Thus far, however, Lula has surprised many of his critics and outraged some supporters by forsaking socialist doctrine. He has managed to gain the confidence of investors with his monetary and fiscal discipline, particularly his willingness to undertake pension reforms. Through a series of eligibility, benefit, and tax adjustments, Lula has reined in the pension system deficit.

The government has been restructuring its debt as a defense against external economic shocks and fluctuating interest rates, while running primary budget surpluses (before interest payments) to stabilize the debt and comply with IMF demands. Nevertheless, the overall debt load continues to expand (as it does in the United States), swelled by high interest payments on the country's massive total borrowings.

Lula finds himself walking a tightrope between efforts to reform the economy and near-term problems caused by the stagnating effects of sky-high interest rates designed to curb inflation. GDP declined last year for the first time in a dozen years and unemployment climbed into double digits. But the President has vowed to stay the course, saying the jobs will follow as production expands and investment increases.

If Brazil can bring its spending under control and convince the public and outside investors that its economic reforms are here to stay, its potential may, at last, become reality. But that is a mighty big "if."

In both Argentina and Brazil, a lack of economic discipline, coupled with the inevitable corruption that takes root when government leaders lose sight of their responsibility to promote the common good, led to decades of economic havoc, crippling the economy and the lives of many of their citizens. What sends shivers down my spine are the unmistakable parallels between the situation we find ourselves in today in the United States and that which typically has preceded a financial collapse in a Third World country: years of large trade and budget deficits; ever-heavier debt loads with an increase in short-term borrowing; tales of accounting scandals and corporate greed; and out-of-control spending—exactly what Americans have seen over the last four years. We ignore the handwriting on the wall at our great peril.

FINANCIAL FOLLY THROUGH HISTORY

The plight of our South American neighbors is perhaps familiar because of its proximity and the press coverage it receives in our own country. The economic lessons of history stretch back as far as there have been rulers, taxes, and government spending.

Before the Roman civilization collapsed, riches rolled in from every corner of its far-flung empire. The fall of Rome had its beginnings in the extravagant behavior of three successive emperors— Caligula, Claudius, and Nero (the fiddler). Each wasted his lavish wealth on showy villas, feasts and orgies, fancy temples, no-show jobs for cronies, and bribes to buy the loyalty of the army and the Praetorian Guard. When they ran out of cash, all reacted in the same disastrous manner: They raised taxes, confiscated the funds of wealthy citizens, and diluted the money supply by melting down old coins to make new ones that contained less gold and silver and more base metal. Predictably enough, the result was severe inflation. In one 30-year period during the third century A.D., for example, the price of a loaf of bread soared from the equivalent of $2 to $2,000—an increase of 100,000 percent.

Inflation was but one nail in Rome's coffin. By the time the empire collapsed, the disastrously high taxes—levied not for productive public works but to permit spending on luxuries—had destroyed Rome's commerce while its cities and towns were reduced to rubble for lack of maintenance and new building. Its dwindling populace was impoverished, and riots and rebellion were commonplace.

Much the same thing happened to Spain 1,300 years later. The wealth of the Indies made it one of the mightiest countries in Europe. But, in an ironic twist, it also contributed to Spain's eventual downfall, as the importation of so much gold and silver drove up price inflation and destabilized Spain's currency. Exacerbating matters were the enormous costs of warfare and a bloated civil service that forced Spain's monarchs to run huge deficits. By the end of the sixteenth century, revenues covered only half the nation's spending. (U.S. tax revenues covered 85 percent of our government's total spending in 2003—but if we exclude the government's borrowing from the Social Security trust fund surplus that was used to pay general expenses, the number drops to 61 percent.) Spanish farming and industry were ground down by murderous taxes, repeated currency devaluations, and the growing inflation. Spain lost its global clout as the empire shrank to a fraction of its former size.

Inflation is never far away when an economic debacle is taking place. But the bout of hyperinflation that preceded the collapse of the Weimar Republic in post–World War I Germany was the worst in recorded history. One of the most vivid images of that era comes from the famous cartoon depiction of a German housewife pushing a wheelbarrow full of currency on her way to buy a loaf of bread. The price of a loaf of rye bread that cost just 0.29 marks in 1914 ran up to 1,200 marks in the summer of 1923 and then to *428 billion* marks in November of that year. So worthless did the German currency become that, rather than buy kindling wood, housewives found it cheaper to use their millions of paper marks to start their kitchen fires.

The postwar fiscal crisis devastated Austria, as well. Preferring to borrow rather than raise taxes during the war, both countries accumulated enormous debts. Their situations became desperate when the Allies, under the misguided Treaty of Versailles, insisted on massive reparations payments.

Austria's budget deficits averaged more than 50 percent of total government spending in the years from 1919 to 1922. It financed these deficits largely by selling bonds to the central bank, which bought them with newly created money—in effect, rubber checks—thus rapidly expanding the money supply. The inevitable result was inflation. In the 11 months from October 1921 through August 1922, the Austrian inflation rate rose 6,990 percent, and the U.S. dollar, which traded for 17 crowns at the start of 1919, was worth 71,000 crowns by December 1922.

To balance its budget and halt the spiraling inflation, the Austrian government slashed the number of government employees, increased taxes, raised the prices of government-sold goods and services, and improved the efficiency of tax collection. As a result, unemployment jumped tenfold in one year and continued to climb for several years until confidence returned and recovery began.

In Germany, the government's deficit rose to 88 percent of revenues by 1923, financed almost entirely by printing money. The Weimar government literally had to requisition printing presses from German publishers to keep up with the demand for new, ever-larger-denomination bills—a 50-million-mark banknote was issued in September 1923. Germany recorded the almost unfathomable hyperinflation of 1.02 trillion percent during the 16 months from August 1922 through November 1923.

Complete anarchy loomed if Germany could not break the back of this extreme inflation. To stabilize the monetary system, the government issued a new currency, the Rentenmark, one of which was equal to 1 billion old marks. The government also slashed its bureaucratic ranks by 25 percent, raised taxes, and pledged not to spend a pfennig more than it took in. The strategy restored price stability, but people were ruined. Savings were destroyed, and pensioners were left essentially destitute. American writer Pearl Buck recorded her impressions after visiting Germany in 1923: "The cities were still there, the houses not yet bombed and in ruins, but the victims were millions of people. They had lost their fortunes, their savings; they were dazed and inflation-shocked and did not understand how it had happened to them and who the foe was who had defeated them. Yet they had lost their self-assurance, their feeling that they themselves could be the masters of their own lives if only they worked hard enough; and lost, too, were the old values of morals, of ethics, of decency." The stage had been set for the rise of Hitler and the Nazi party.

In every economic disaster, we see the same forces at work: year after year of spending more than a government takes in, the inexorable buildup of debt that slows a nation's progress. Rather than investing in desperately needed infrastructure, industry, and efficient government administration, huge portions of national resources are tied up in debt service, entitlement programs, and subsidies.

And that is what has been going on in the United States in recent decades. Our national debt rose from 34 percent of GDP in 1980 to 62 percent in 2003, a figure that exceeds Argentina's ratio of debt to GDP in 1999. On its current growth track of 7 percent a year, our debt will pass 100 percent of GDP in 2024—unless we come to our senses.

We are already paying a price for these excesses. Again, our annual budget deficit now stands at 4.5 percent of GDP, a rate that far outpaces our national savings rate; we finance the deficit only by borrowing from foreigners. Our grandchildren will be stuck with the bill. If we do not quickly reverse our headlong plunge into debt, we risk crushing interest rates, rising inflation, a shortage of capital, and massive unemployment. Beyond that lurk the lessons of Rome and the Weimar Republic: hyperinflation and anarchy.

A CALL TO ARMS

At least some of the remedies to the problems we face are plain to see. But staying the course when the inevitable crises arise will take a leader with a strong backbone, one able to withstand extreme pressure from every corner. One who has the support of a bipartisan majority of American citizens.

But first, we must convince those already in power, and those who hope to be, that we will no longer tolerate business as usual in our nation's capital. That we want nothing less than a new culture of fiscal responsibility? Chapter 11 suggests what must be done and how our government can get mobilized to confront our fiscal crisis before it's too late.

AMERICA THE SOLVENT AND PROSPEROUS

WHEN HARD TIMES hit, I believe most people know what to do. They pull in their belts. They figure out which things they can afford to keep buying and which they have to cut back on or eliminate altogether. It's not fun to go without: without a vacation trip, a new stove, a dinner out, or new shoes. But people do what they have to.

The same is true for corporations. Over the last decade, hundreds of some of our biggest companies have undertaken painful restructurings, rooting out inefficiencies, reducing overhead in general and unnecessary jobs in particular: Kodak, IBM, GM, Time Warner. It wasn't fun, but everyone knew it had to be done, that circumstances demanded hard choices.

Our federal government is the exception to the rule. When the government gets in trouble financially and needs to rethink its priorities, downsize its bureaucracy, and tighten its belt, our presidents and congressional representatives simply ignore the obvious and continue the same irresponsible behavior that created the problem in the first place. They go right on racking up huge debts, postponing a day of reckoning as long as possible.

As this book has made clear, America has a serious problem, one that will soon derail our economy and our country if we don't deal with it *now*. Given the horrendous size of our public debt, and the record-breaking annual deficits that feed it, we are on the edge of the abyss. If the deficits were temporary in nature—caused solely by our response to 9/11—we could probably grow our way out of them without mortgaging our future. But these deficits are part of our government's mind-set. They are long-term, they are escalating, and they are an economic time bomb waiting to explode. Today, our nation's future hangs on how the President and Congress choose to deal with the threat. But to date, there is no sign from President Bush, his domestic or economic advisers, or Congress that they even recognize the problem, much less that they have the will and the courage to take bold steps to solve it.

Over the last 20 years, our elected representatives have made occasional efforts to rein in their profligate spending. They have even succeeded at times, providing a precedent our current leaders can follow. The Gramm-Rudman-Hollings Balanced Budget and Emergency Control Act of 1985, for instance, required that Congress and the President meet responsible fiscal targets; if they failed, automatic spending cuts took effect. But a Supreme Court ruling blunted the measure's teeth, and Congress made sure the budget remained unbalanced.

The most effective piece of legislation, the Budget Enforcement Act (BEA) of 1990, set annual limits on discretionary spending and required the government to follow a pay-as-you-go procedure. Known as Pay-Go, it required that any new spending or tax cuts be offset by equivalent spending cuts or tax increases. These tough measures, together with extensions and revisions passed in 1993 and 1997 and a rise in taxes and a strong economy, worked to reduce and then actually eliminate the budget deficit. As I noted earlier, President Clinton presided over the largest single paydown of the federal debt in U.S. history. It was an important first step—but Congress treated it as if it were victory itself. Since the law's expiration at the end of fiscal 2002, a Republican-controlled Congress has beaten back repeated efforts to renew it. And spending, of course, has exploded.

It will take a renewal of the legislation to impose fiscal discipline on Congress and the President. Even then, however, as aptly noted by the Congressional Budget Office, "No procedures to control the deficits or impose budgetary restraint will ever be effective in the absence of an overall political consensus to achieve these goals." Therefore, our first goal is to convince our leaders, Republicans and Democrats alike, that ensuring our country's financial future is the single most important issue facing our great country today. Only then will Washington take our fiscal crisis seriously and push to balance the budget and call a halt to expanding debt.

Our leaders cannot be excused for the mess in which America now finds itself. We must demand that they come to their senses and confront the problems before it's too late. I've created a list of suggested actions they should take, followed by ideas about how our government can best get itself mobilized to act.

SHRINK THE DEBT

Our $7.3 trillion national debt, more than $24,000 for every man, woman, and child in the country, is obscene. Ideally, it should be paid down entirely. But in today's climate, that may be too much to ask. At a bare minimum, we must insist that the President and Congress hold the debt at its current level. That means eliminating the annual deficits. And I mean eliminating them, painful as that might be. Merely reducing the deficits would be like applying a Band-Aid to a gaping wound. With a consistently balanced budget, economic growth could lower our national debt from its current level of 62 percent of gross domestic product—the highest in 50 years—to 40 percent of GDP. That would return the debt to its proportional size through most of our history. A debt that size would be less likely to be a drag on our economy, or a sword hanging over our heads.

Should we fail to shrink the debt (relative to GDP) immediately, a significant increase in the rock-bottom interest rate we now pay on our debt could send our economy into free fall. The CBO estimates that a rise of a mere 1 percent in interest rates would add $592 billion to the national debt over 10 years. A sharp rise in the price of oil or other commodities could send consumer prices soaring and force the Federal Reserve to raise interest rates to stave off inflation. Or our overseas lenders could balk at buying Treasuries, forcing the government to increase rates to lure them back or attract new lenders.

BALANCE THE BUDGET

To reduce our debt, the federal government needs to balance its annual budget. Period. No more loading today's costs onto the backs of our grandchildren. I won't kid you. There is no easy or painless way to reduce the annual deficit. Realistically, given its record-high levels, it probably won't be eliminated in a year or two. But it *must* be eliminated more quickly than in the 1990s. After the security of the country itself, it must be our highest priority. Our leaders, and we as citizens, must be willing to accept whatever sacrifices that entails. To begin with, we must set a firm target date to balance the budget, reducing deficits to zero in three years. And once that is achieved, we must outlaw what has become the automatic, year-after-year raising of what now passes for a ceiling on the national debt. Absent a genuine crisis such as a larger war, Congress must commit itself to cutting costs and doing whatever is necessary on the tax-revenue side to stop increasing our already historic level of debt.

Sometimes a nation can get lucky. A sudden spurt in productivity or consumer spending can produce unexpected revenues. In the past, such windfalls have, by and large, been spent, applied to the funding of new public services or programs. Or they have inspired leaders such as Ronald Reagan and George W. Bush to give us new tax cuts. We can no longer afford such luxuries. We must do even better than Pay-Go, which permitted new spending and tax cuts if they were offset elsewhere. Our nation is teetering on the abyss because of our reckless fiscal policies. To correct our course, any extra revenues must be dedicated to shrinking the deficit and, if possible, reducing the total debt.

CUT SPENDING

Over the past five years, mandatory spending in the budget (interest payments on the debt plus entitlement programs) has risen at an average annual rate of 7 percent, while discretionary spending (everything else) has jumped by an average of 10 percent a year. This is truly voodoo economics, and it's impossible to sustain. Studies have shown that to balance the budget, we must hold the growth of both mandatory and discretionary spending to 3 percent *or less.*

Make no mistake, cutting the growth of mandatory spending so sharply will be a Herculean task. Inevitably, interest on the debt will increase, since at today's rock-bottom levels, rates have nowhere to go but up. And the total debt will continue to rise *until* we balance the budget. The looming retirement of the baby-boom generation, which begins in earnest in 2012, guarantees that even if benefits are cut sharply, total entitlement spending on Social Security, Medicare, and Medicaid benefits will go up.

I believe, as painful as it is, that there's no alternative to cutting benefits. The trick is to do it as gently and fairly as possible, while still obtaining big results.

In past years, it was politically impossible to calibrate Social Security and Medicare benefits by income levels (making them more generous for poor pensioners and lower for people who can afford to pay their own way). But 2003 legislation broke this taboo on Medicare with a new graduated tax on its Part B benefits. Hats off to Congress on that one. The principle should now be applied across the board to Medicare and Social Security, phased in over the next decade in fairness to those already retired.

Higher-income wage earners should get reduced—even sharply reduced—Social Security benefits. The original Social Security program was never intended to pay their way. In return, legislators could offer tax incentives to encourage them to step up their savings, so that they wind up with the same level of income in retirement at a much lower cost to the government.

The original retirement age of 65 was set at a time when only 40 percent of the workforce was expected to live that long. Given our vastly greater longevity today, the retirement age is already being raised, in graduated steps, to 67. We should extend it to 70. If this sounds unfair to older people, think of this: Even with a later retirement age, they will still collect benefits for many years more than the program's founders ever contemplated. And if we don't raise the retirement age, the burden will fall squarely on the shoulders of our children and our children's children.

There's more. Social Security benefits are currently indexed for inflation and wage growth, but the formulas being used overcompensate. The initial benefit base is linked not to prices but to wages, which have historically risen faster than the cost of living by about 1 percent annually. Changing the benefit base formula to a price index, as Britain has already done, would save hundreds of billions of dollars in the next few decades. The impact would be felt only gradually, and beneficiaries would still be protected from inflation.

Politically sensitive though it may be, we must also rethink the Medicare prescription-drug benefit passed by Congress in 2003. Why? Its costs will be measured in trillions—and Congress and the President have set *nothing* at all aside to pay them. The first decade's cost, belatedly disclosed as $534 billion, escalates to *$1 trillion* in the second decade, and almost $2 trillion in the third. Even people covered by the new bill have decried it as a giveaway to the drug companies. Our debt-and-deficit predicament provides Congress with the perfect cover to kill the law. The fact is, we can't afford it. Failing outright repeal, the lawmakers must amend the law to create a more affordable program—and with provisions for funding it.

None of these cuts in entitlements will be easy, nor will they be popular. Enacting such cuts must be done in a bipartisan way, with both Democrats and Republicans uniting for the public good. It will take ingenuity, commitment, and courage. Perhaps more palatable alternatives will present themselves. But some form of sharp entitlement cuts is a stark necessity, and Americans must be helped to understand that.

With regard to discretionary spending, Congress and the President must trim programs across the board. Along with the debt, the size of the government bureaucracy has soared in recent years. There are simply too many people on the payroll performing unnecessary or overlapping functions. The private sector has saved billions of dollars by streamlining its operations. It's time for the public sector to follow suit.

One of the hard lessons businesses have learned lately is the value of outsourcing any activities that other organizations can do better and/or less expensively. It was a hard lesson because corporate leaders' ego and pride was involved. Government leaders have their own version of such false pride. Agency heads gauge their importance largely by their head count; they hate to see their turf reduced. They will fiercely battle any suggestion that a nongovernment organization might be better equipped to do some aspect of their job. They particularly oppose privatizing any part of their domain.

The urgent need to eliminate annual deficits presents us with an opportunity to revisit the privatization option. When we do, I think we'll find it makes sense. As the Grace Commission—charged by President Reagan with ferreting out government waste—noted in 1984, "The government's business is not to be in business."

Probably the most impressive example of a nation getting its fiscal house in order came when Britain reduced its national debt from 51 percent of GDP in 1979 to 27 percent 11 years later. That was accomplished, in part, through the sale of state-owned companies. Privatization of U.S. government assets would yield huge sums for use in reducing the red ink. Beyond that, it would help balance the budget by erasing the regular losses chalked up by those assets.

We have no major government industries to be sold off. But we could sell some federal land and follow Canada's lead by privatizing our air traffic controllers. We could and probably should privatize the Tennessee Valley Authority (TVA), the multibillion-dollar utility run by the federal government. Privatizing would force TVA to become more efficient. It would cut the government's spending and raise federal revenues by increasing the corporate tax base. We should also force Amtrak to stand on its own feet or fold. The best way to do that is to sell it—if we can find anyone willing to buy. Of course, any proposed privatization would have to be carefully evaluated to make sure the job would be better done privately.

One possible means of shrinking the government would be to begin a policy of "sunsetting," automatically terminating agencies and programs after a set number of years unless they are expressly reauthorized. A Sunset Commission could be established to review federal programs on a 12-year rotating basis, recommending whether to abolish them or not. Wasteful, unneeded, and poorly run programs would be slated for reform, privatization, or elimination. Sound Draconian? Remember that in the private sector, divisions and even companies are routinely "sunsetted"—put out of business by rivals that better serve consumers, the public. Roughly 10 percent of all U.S. companies go out of business each year. Yet federal agencies live forever—and for the most part *grow*—no matter how inefficient, obsolete, or useless they may be.

HANDS OFF

Here are some of the commonplace practices—additions, really—our government has fallen prey to that we must, going forward, avoid at all costs.

- *Raiding the trust funds.* Our government has continually siphoned off revenues from the government trust funds for decades, virtually since their creation, and used them for expenses we couldn't otherwise fund. Rather than building up the trust funds with real dollars, as founders of the funds intended, our politicians—both Republicans and Democrats—have filled them with a slew of worthless rubber checks—nonmarketable government IOUs and empty promises. With the urgent need to balance the budget, Congress will be sorely tempted to continue this. I say the hijacking must stop immediately. It is fraud, plain and simple. We must find real revenues to replace the borrowed trust funds—or cut back on the programs we don't have the money to pay for—just as you and I would with our household budgets. Moreover, the government must find a way to put back into the funds, on a reasonable schedule, the nearly $1.5 trillion it has taken in past years.

- *Making loans.* It's time to get the government out of the lending business. When federal agencies bail out companies with loans or loan guarantees, the government ends up on the short end. In the case of the savings-and-loan crisis in the 1980s, for example, government backing of failed banks cost the taxpayers more than $500 billion in payments to depositors. In addition, the loans made by such agencies as Fannie Mae, Freddie Mac, the Veterans Administration, and the Small Business Administration are explicitly or implicitly underwritten by our government. Inevitably, any default will be added to the ever-rising mountain of our national debt. Nothing justifies this risk when our own government is in such peril.

- *Raising the tax rate.* The idea is appealing: Let's climb out of the hole we've dug by raising tax rates and using those new revenues to get rid of our debt. Forget it. Higher taxes have a way of putting a damper on economic growth, and slower growth inevitably reduces tax revenues. So you end up back where you started—or even worse off, since the new tax money typically never gets applied to debt reduction. That's not to say we can't find ways of increasing revenues. But we should do it by broadening the tax base, not raising tax rates.

The first target should be tax evasion, which has been on the rise in recent years. Our system of taxation depends heavily on voluntary compliance; people who think their neighbors are getting away with cheating become cynical—and far more ready to try it, too.

Estimates of the revenues lost to tax evasion run into the hundreds of billions. Yet Congress has consistently starved the Internal Revenue Service of funds for auditors and enforcement people, despite the fact that everyone acknowledges that each additional enforcement officer returns the government many times his or her annual salary.

Another place the tax base needs strengthening? Corporate taxes. The army of business lobbyists has been so effective at twisting our representatives' arms that loopholes for their clients abound. A dismal 60 percent of U.S. businesses paid *no federal income tax at all* last year. Those that did pay got *enormous breaks.* Ostensibly, corporations pay 35 percent of their profits after allowable deductions. But the reality is far more telling: Nine out of ten corporations paid less than *5 percent.* Once again, enforcement is lax at best. The IRS is reliably reported to have no collection personnel at all in its compliance division handling medium and large businesses; the collection people focus their work in the self-employed small-business division. The bottom line? Revenues from corporate taxes, which once came to 40 percent of all federal revenues, have fallen to 7.5 percent. Our corporations are essentially receiving a free ride on the backs of middle-class taxpaying citizens (and more than a few corporations have established their world headquarters offshore so that they can avoid any income tax at all). That is a scandal. Congress must close the loopholes, ramp up enforcement, and overhaul the system in a way that makes corporations pay their fair share.

- *Devaluation.* On the face of it, lowering the value of the dollar by printing more dollars solves many of our problems. Suddenly, because they are cheaper, American goods become more attractive to overseas customers, reducing our trade deficit. Our goods also compete better with imports in our domestic markets. But the arguments against devaluation are stronger. For one thing, it leads to inflation, slashing the buying power of Joe Citizen. Moreover, devaluation wouldn't give the economy that much of a boost: Our country's manufacturing capacity is so diminished that only 12 percent of American jobs these days are in manufacturing. Moreover, our trading partners would be furious if we deliberately sank the dollar, likely putting up more barriers to our exports.

AN ACTION PLAN

To successfully attack our national insolvency, our leaders must understand the absolute necessity of doing so and unite in their support. What do I mean by that? For openers, the President has to rally the public to the cause—not an easy assignment, given the lies and half-truths Washington has used for so many years to gloss over the size and the danger of our indebtedness. The President and Congress—and the leaders of both parties—must treat this issue as critical to the survival of our way of life. Virtually every president has officially called for a drastic cutback in the growth of our national debt. Now the President—whoever he is—must walk the walk. Finally, we the public must make it clear to the President and Congress alike that we will vote against any politician who strays from the path of solvency and debt reduction. We must save our country.

In the midterm election of 1994, many newly elected Republican members of Congress signed a "Contract with America," pledging to work to reduce the growth in government spending and bring the budget into balance. Amazingly, working with a Democratic president, that's just what they did! Let's ask those running for election this year to sign another Contract with America, a contract to eliminate the deficit, balance the budget, and tackle the desperate problems of Social Security and Medicare. Tackling these kinds of tough, unpopular issues, rising above the fray of partisan politics for the good of the country, is what real leadership is all about.

Given the scope of the challenge, we would need a special team of talented, dedicated managers to put such a contract into effect. The President and Congress should draw them from the ranks of business, finance, and the professions. In a fine old tradition, I would pay them just a dollar a year—for there could be no real recompense for such selfless service. One possible model might be the Manhattan Project, the code name for the research effort that led to the creation of the first atomic bomb. Call this project Return to Sanity.

The campaign should operate on two levels. One group would work directly with the President and Congress, picking targets and breaking through political roadblocks. These experts in diplomacy and crisis management would have the unenviable task of dealing with recalcitrant politicians and special-interest groups. They would have no power of their own, but the spotlight they shined on a project would, in effect, ensure that our leaders kept their promises to reform.

This is not easy stuff. It would involve sacrifice for all of us. In such a campaign, virtually every American would feel the pinch. No federal program would be immune from the cost-cutting shears. The complaints and pleas from voters, special-interest groups, and lobbyists would be loud and numerous. But if enough general zeal for reform could be focused on Washington, such individual protests could be overridden.

The second group of volunteer managers, by far the larger, would drill down into the bureaucracy, finding ways to trim budgets and squeeze out costs. These accountants and efficiency experts would spot waste and stamp it out, search out overlapping jobs and redundant layers of management and eliminate them. Old programs that had never met their goals would be canceled. New programs that had grown far beyond expectations would be pruned.

Before finishing their work, these managers would prepare a set of guidelines for government leaders to prevent another gross buildup of the national debt. Congress and the President could create a new, independent watchdog agency charged with sounding a public alarm when economic developments pose a threat, or when our politicians, swayed by self-interest, start to stray from the path of fiscal restraint.

Before disbanding, the managers would need to set up a mechanism for holding Congress and the President accountable for fiscal discipline. Perhaps Congress, working with the administration, could draft a law modeled on the Sarbanes-Oxley bill, passed in the wake of the recent corporate scandals to hold businesspeople's feet to the fire. Just as CEOs must now sign off on their financial statements under pain of prosecution, so our elected officials should have to read and be held accountable for the budgets they pass and the long-term consequences of the programs they inflict on us.

DRIVING A DREAM

What I'm suggesting is no mere political reform or citizens' campaign, aimed to pass a law or two and then quietly subside. Rather, we need a crusade—one in which the goal is to achieve a revolutionary, permanent sea-change in the Washington way of life. And it is a sad measure of the critical need for change that it must take a revolution to return honesty, responsibility, and good governance to government.

Imagine, for a moment, a Washington where Democrats and Republicans stop their political party posturing and maneuvering and bring a sense of bipartisan good faith to their dealings with the budget. Imagine an end to the accounting gimmickry, the hidden revenue transfers, and the flat-out lies pushed on us as economic projections that now hide the real costs of running government.

Imagine a government that actually lives by its own rules. There are dozens of rules governing the budget process; both houses of Congress, for instance, require that members be given a minimum of three days to read any budget bill before voting on it. But in January 2004, as in 2003, most of the year's appropriations bills were bundled into a vast omnibus bill totaling more than 3,000 pages—and the rule was waived. Members had just a few hours to absorb it all. Thousands of pork-barrel projects totaling $22.9 billion weren't even noticed except by their sponsors.

What we need is a kind of religious conversion. We need Washington to revert to the spirit of our founding fathers. They, too, were far from perfect: They had their own agendas, they horse-traded and gerrymandered, and they dealt deviously with opposing factions at times. But they believed in their hearts that they were building a great nation and had a larger duty to that cause. As our founders once did, our politicians and all Americans must learn to think for the long term, rather than just the next election cycle. We must promote public debate by airing our long-range strategies. And we must find leaders with the courage to do what's needed for the long-term good of our country—even if that means touching an occasional political third rail that stands in the way.

The runaway national debt represents a clear and present danger for America. There are undoubtedly other ways to deal with some of the issues other than the ones I've suggested here. At the end of the day, my concern is less about how we go about fending off disaster than that we get started quickly and resolutely. There is no time to waste. But how do we get there from here? The next chapter spells out how we can use the strength of our democracy to ensure that our voices are heard.

CHAPTER 12

THE BUCK STARTS HERE

AFTER HAVING READ so far in this book, are you mad? Are you ready to denounce government leaders for their outrageous abuses of power? I hope so. The President and our elected representatives are ruining our country. Yet neither the Bush Administration nor incumbent senators and congressmen and -women will admit error. It will take all the grit we can muster to restore sane policies and save the American Dream from oblivion.

The enormity of the problem—all $7.3 trillion of it—is crystal clear. And so is the solution: We have to direct the bulk of our energies toward reducing spending and reducing the debt. All that's missing is a call to arms for our President and Congress to act.

The mess we find ourselves in derives from decades of folly— wrong assumptions, misguided policies, partisan politics, to say nothing of deliberate deception by leaders of both parties. Fiscal irresponsibility is the norm in Washington. And the determination of our current political leaders to cut taxes and bloat spending has sent us over the edge. Is it likely government wastrels will see the light and become paragons of thrift?

All of us must treat this crisis as a national emergency, for that is most certainly what it is. If we join hands and voices in common cause, if we vote for strong-willed leaders who have the courage to do the right thing for the good of the United States, we can save our country. Those in Congress fear nothing so much as losing their seat of power. Majority rule governs this country; let's reach out and create a majority. Together, we can end the abuses that are undermining our nation. We must show that millions of Americans are wise to Washington's con games and that we won't tolerate them a minute longer.

In the final analysis, only immense public outcry and protest can halt our deadly deficit-and-debt spiral. In other words, the buck starts here, with you and me.

I can hear readers asking, "What can I do? I'm just one person." The answer: Plenty. As Margaret Mead once said, "Never doubt that a small group of thoughtful, committed people can change the world. Indeed, it is the only thing that ever has."

It's easy to rationalize that democracy is a fraud: You can't beat city hall. But that's a truth riddled with exceptions. For one thing, crooked politicians have a way of overreaching, of finally stealing one dime too many. For another, the last half-century has demonstrated as never before that individual Americans, alone and in groups, can bend the government to their will. They have organized marches and rallies, flooded Congress with their phone calls and letters, and recently leveraged the Internet to raise huge sums to support their causes.

Elected representatives pay attention when you make an effort to voice your opinion. They have to. They're in the business of getting reelected, and they need your vote to stay in business. The President and his staff in the White House count the calls, letters, and e-mails they receive. They do the same thing over at the House of Representatives and the Senate. Candidates for public office can't afford to ignore the public, and they don't.

We have to pressure our government leaders to make them truly believe our warning: "You will be out of a job if you don't act on our concerns." Only huge voter pressure will force them to stop deficit spending and pour all energy and available resources into slashing the national debt. But it won't happen unless all of us take concrete steps to move the issue to the top of the political agenda. This chapter suggests how we can go about it.

CHOOSE YOUR ROLE

Each avenue of protest available to you has its distinct advantages. As an individual, for example, you can freely tailor the message you send to our leaders in Washington to suit your own voice and beliefs. You can express feelings of disappointment or anger without the constraints sometimes imposed by the policies or personnel of an existing group.

Most techniques that groups employ can also be used by an individual protester. True, your single voice will not resonate as strongly as that of a group. But it will be heard. Write letters and e-mails, or call your congressperson, your senators, and even the wallahs of the White House. Study the issues and discuss them at meetings of local organizations to which you belong. Most important, vote for candidates who support your concerns about the economy and the deficit, those who understand the insolvency threat and will fight to end misguided budget deficits and cut the national debt. When this issue becomes key to getting elected, more and more candidates will listen to and respect your concerns.

To amplify your individual actions, support one of the existing organizations dedicated to government efficiency and fiscal responsibility. Or start your own grassroots movement. You can easily check out an existing group by Googling its name or sampling its Web site to see if its focus and efforts dovetail with yours. (Contact information for a number of such groups is provided below.) When you find one that fits, give it all the time and financial support you can. Choose a group with a proven track record for pushing an agenda at the right time and place to maximize its impact. Again, nothing beats the power of numbers in electoral politics. When any group creates a vast chorus of voters' voices, it acquires real power to pressure decision makers in Washington. The AARP is a perfect example.

Concord Coalition
1011 Arlington Boulevard
Suite 330

Arlington, VA 22209
Telephone: 703-894-6222
Fax: 703-894-6231
Web site: www.concordcoalition.org
E-mail: concordcoalition@concordcoalition.org

Citizens Against Government Waste
1301 Connecticut Avenue NW
Suite 400
Washington, DC 20036
Telephone: 1-202-467-5300
Web site: www.cagw.org
E-mail: membership@cagw.org

Taxpayers for Common Sense
651 Pennsylvania Avenue SE
Washington, DC 20003
Telephone: 1-202-546-8500 or
Toll free: 1-800-TAXPAYER (1-800-829-7293)
Web site: www.taxpayer.net
E-mail: info@taxpayer.net

Citizens for a Sound Economy
1523 16th Street NW, 2nd Floor
Washington, DC 20036
Telephone: 1-202-783-3870 or Toll free: 1-888-JOIN CSE
(1-888-564-6273)
Web site: www.cse.org
E-mail: cse@cse.org

Americans for Tax Reform
1920 L Street NW
Suite 200
Washington, DC 20036

Telephone: 1-202-785-0266
Web site: www.atr.org
E-mail: friends@atr.org

To build your own grassroots movement, share your knowledge of the issues with friends and relatives. Recruit friends and family members to send letters or e-mails to the President and your local congressional representatives. Draft a sample letter you can send to others you know, encouraging them to use it to compose their own letters. In my experience in dealing with Washington, if you want to pierce its defenses, one vivid personal letter will often outweigh a truckload of form letters.

The Internet has made it much easier to put together this kind of temporary organization. E-mail a dozen people and invite them to join your write-in campaign. If each of the 12 forwards the message to another dozen, and so on, you can quickly amass hundreds, if not thousands, of potential voters. E-mail also makes the task of typing and forwarding your message much easier.

You can also start your own grassroots organization aimed at pressuring Washington. Again, begin with people you know, explaining in person or by e-mail your concern about the dangers of deficit spending and the runaway national debt. Expand your reach with notices on office or community bulletin boards. If you're comfortable speaking in public, graduate to a presentation in community forums. Look for friendly town libraries, civic-minded clubs, recreation centers, adult-education programs—any podium that welcomes local citizens with lively ideas. Listeners who share your concerns relish working with like-minded neighbors. Once you have a solid base of sympathizers, you can officially organize, selecting a name, electing officers, and adopting one or more of the actionable approaches described in the following pages.

Only you can decide how deeply you can or want to get involved. Be aware that it takes a lot of time, energy, and confidence to put together an action group from scratch. If you persuade 10 people who each recruit 10 more, you're acting as a multiplier, ensuring that your concerns reach countless others. To combat the potential catastrophe of our exploding debt, we need thousands of multipliers and then some. The stakes are huge—nothing less than saving our nation from economic collapse.

CHOOSE YOUR TARGET

The first step in preparing for battle in this process is to master the congressional budget process. That's where our leaders decide the size of the annual deficit—and ignore the skyrocketing national debt. That's where we must focus our political firepower.

The budget process is remarkably unwieldy—tailor-made for deficit financing. For starters, no one ever decides exactly how much will be spent. Instead, a jumble of 17 House committees and 15 Senate committees develop their own separate spending bills for the agencies and programs under their jurisdiction. The inevitable scrounging for ever-bigger chunks of our tax revenues gets pretty grubby, to say the least. With every federal agency importuning its congressional overseers for funds, and every lobbyist working on susceptible committee members, the annual Treasury raid has at times resembled buzzards feasting on roadkill.

Obviously, you can't talk to every member of all 32 committees, so you've got to cherry-pick among them. Focus on the committees where your representative or senators serve; those from your own state or district have more reason to pay attention to you—remember, they want your vote—than do other members of Congress. Or focus on committees that deal with matters in which you have some experience or expertise (in which case you should contact the committee chairman).

Your primary goal (could anything be more patriotic?) is to influence committee members and their staffs to move in the direction of responsible fiscal behavior. To identify and contact them, consult *The Congressional Directory,* an annual publication available at local libraries. Or order your own copy from the Government Printing Office by mail or through its Web site. Contact:

U.S. Government Printing Office
Mail Stop: SDE
732 North Capitol Street NW
Washington, DC 20401
Telephone: 1-888-293-6498
E-mail: www.gpoaccess.gov

Wherever you choose to focus your attention, you need to find out exactly when those committees hold hearings on specific bills, or when the bills they approve are due for later consideration by the full House or Senate. The budget process has its own schedule.

Each February, about eight months before the beginning of the federal government's fiscal year on October 1, the President submits his budget to Congress. Committees and subcommittees of both houses have until April 15 to put together a budget resolution. The resolution sets forth the amount of money the government expects to receive and spend over the next five fiscal years without spelling out the numbers for specific programs.

Come summer, the federal agencies submit their individual budgets to Congress, where Senate and House committees work out revenue and spending levels for the coming fiscal year. Meanwhile, the agencies plead their cases with both Congress and the President.

You want to hit key lawmakers with your calls or e-mails precisely when they're making crucial decisions. Timing is everything. No matter how convincing your arguments, they're worthless if you make them too early or too late. Pinpoint the decisive moment when Congress teeters between duty and deceit. Strike then, and only then.

For online information about the various House and Senate appropriations subcommittee meetings, go to http://appropriations.senate.gov and http://appropriations.house.gov. The *Federal Register*, published daily, is another reliable source of information on congressional hearings and data relating to federal regulations and agency activities. You can read it at the library or access it online at www. gpoaccess.gov/fr/index.html. You or your group can also subscribe through the Government Printing Office.

To prepare your argument, you might look over the record of previous years' hearings and committee reports. To find them, contact the Senate Budget Committee at 1-202-224-0642 or online at www. senate.gov/~budget, and the House Budget Committee at 1-202-226-7270 or www.house.gov/budget. For a copy of a bill, contact the district offices of your senators or representative.

To follow the progress of a piece of legislation through the labyrinthine budget process, you can also consult the *Congressional Record*, a description of day-by-day activity on the floor of Congress. It can be read in the library, and the *Record* going back to 1994 can be viewed online at www.gpoaccess.gov/crecord/index.html. You can also subscribe through the Government Printing Office.

For good measure—modesty will get you nowhere—don't forget to share your views with the President. Besides originating the budget and having the power to veto the final version, the President, as the leader of his political party, wields *great* influence over legislators who share his political beliefs and desire to maintain control of the White House.

CHOOSE YOUR WEAPON

Once you determine the role you want to play and which government officials to focus on, the next step is deciding the best way to make your views known. Methods range from snail mail to e-mail, from personal visits to media campaigns—each of which I'll discuss momentarily.

Whatever your method, don't be shy—state your case forcefully. Don't apologize for bothering the President or your representative or senator. You may well encounter Capitol Hill elected officials or staff who treat you like a supplicant at some feudal court. You're no such thing. You're a free American on a serious mission. Remember, these people work for you. They're public servants, accountable to you and every other voter in your state or district, and to the nation as a whole. They owe you not just a hearing but a considered response. Of course, that doesn't entitle you to be rude. No matter how angry you are over the government's fiscal idiocies, remain cool and courteous—impressively so. Tirades make only enemies; now is the moment to wow your legislators with the power of your argument and the firmness of your conviction.

Here are some specific pointers to help you make the most of your contacts with your elected representatives and their staffs.

- *Write.* Letters are the traditional method of communication with the President and members of Congress, but times have changed. E-mail is not only easier for the sender, it's easier on the recipient; most congresspersons prefer it to mail that arrives through the U.S. Postal Service. Legislators' e-mail addresses are available on these sites: www.senate.gov and www.house.gov/MemberWWW.html. However, if you prefer to send a letter by regular mail, consult *The Congressional Directory* or call the local offices of your senators and representatives for mailing addresses.

To make President George W. Bush personally aware that you, Voter A. B. Jones, are appalled at the government's reckless course—runaway spending, unconscionable debt, potential bankruptcy—contact him at:

The White House
1600 Pennsylvania Avenue NW
Washington, DC 20500
Telephone: 1-202-456-1111
Fax: 1-202-456-2461
E-mail: president@whitehouse.gov

Whether you choose the pen or the PC, make sure to include your name, address, and phone number. Nobody heeds unsigned

messages. Putting yourself on record gets attention, perhaps respect-
ful attention. If the recipient has any political sense, you'll also get an
answer. Even if it's one of those innocuous White House form letters,
rest assured that somebody tallying public opinion has included
yours. Keep your message brief, no more than 300 words or so. If you
are writing about a specific piece of legislation, be sure to include the
bill number or the name by which it is generally known.

Your first paragraph should state the reason you are sending the
letter. Be concise and to the point. In the body of the letter, lay out
your argument in detail. But, again, stay on message—no rambling.
The last paragraph or two should contain your demand for action.

Here's a sample letter to guide you:

Dear Representative/Senator Jones:
As a voter in your district, I am greatly concerned by your
failure to support efforts to drastically reduce the federal deficit
and national debt. They threaten the future of my family and
the country as a whole, and I am disappointed that you have
not given this matter your highest priority.

Every year, the Congress and President push the debt
higher. Every year, the interest on the debt eats up more and
more of the funds that should be spent on services for your
constituents. Vital programs are being cut back because
Congress lacks the courage to halt its spendthrift behavior and
start acting in a fiscally responsible manner.

The deficits and debt have made us vulnerable to disaster
in many ways. What happens if the foreign investors who hold
40 percent of our debt decide against lending us more money
or begin to sell off the Treasury bonds they already own?
What happens if the economy starts to boom and we enter an
inflationary period?

You know the answer. These all-too-likely events would
send interest rates soaring to the point where payments on the
debt would eat up half or more of the government's discre-

tionary tax revenues. What would you do then? What taxes would you raise? What programs would you cut?

It is past time for you and your colleagues to get serious about the debt crisis. It is not a partisan political issue and must not be treated as such. Deficit financing has to be stopped in its tracks. A share of future revenues must be committed to debt reduction. Now, as hearings begin on H. R. XYZ, I urge you to stop playing roulette with the lives of your constituents and speak out against today's reckless fiscal policies. I look forward to hearing from you on this vital matter.

- *Visit.* Your elected representatives are busy, but not so busy they can't make time to meet with their constituents, either in Washington or in their district offices. Call the district office in your area and make an appointment.

Letters can be very effective, but a personal visit gives you far more clout. It sets you apart as someone willing to devote significant time and energy to your cause, someone who won't be satisfied with a form letter or vague response. In addition, the encounter immediately becomes interactive—you learn your legislators' reasoning and views, and they learn yours, firsthand. It can also lead to a continuing relationship.

Prepare for the meeting by educating yourself on the facts and figures of the debt debate. Compile questions to explore the legislator's views: How seriously does he or she view the deficit-debt problem? How would the legislator balance the budget—cut spending, boost taxes, or both? To what extent, if any, should entitlement programs be privatized? You might consult the Concord Coalition's list of key questions to ask candidates about the budget, Social Security, and Medicare (online at www.concordcoalition.org). Bear in mind that legislators don't necessarily know a lot about the big picture unless they serve on one of the budget committees. So you may actually be able to influence their views.

Even though a district office may be more convenient for you, a meeting in Washington allows you to engage your representatives in their political lairs, the workplace where most of their deals and decisions are made. If a lawmaker is overbooked and can't see you in the near future, don't give up. Make an appointment with one of his or her legislative aides. They often know more about issues than their bosses, because they prepare amendments and stay abreast of new developments. Moreover, the legislator expects them to report on meetings with constituents like you. In fact, if you're in Washington, you can probably get to see a legislative aide just by visiting your representative's office. Though security needs are complicating walk-in visits, and an aide may not be instantly available, the odds are good that staff people will do their best to welcome you. After all, you're a customer.

At the meeting, make it quite clear that you are firmly committed to the fight and will hold the legislator personally responsible for doing something to solve the problem. In other words, this is not a debating society. Even as you listen politely to your legislator's views, you will leave no doubt about the message you are there to deliver: "The debt crisis must be addressed immediately. It represents a clear and present danger to the nation. I hold you, my legislator, responsible for taking action against this threat."

- *Go public.* As an individual or as a member of a group, you can greatly extend your reach by writing letters to the editor of your newspaper or sending informative articles and press releases to your local media, speaking out on the issue in public forums, and organizing demonstrations or petition drives. Each option has its own rules and requirements.

When approaching the media, whether newspapers and magazines or radio and TV shows, remember that space and time are at a premium. To increase your chances of being published or getting airtime, your communications need to be brief and to the point. You should also link them to a recent news story or editorial, preferably one just published. Few media are interested in yesterday's news, much less last week's.

For example, wait to write to a newspaper until it carries an article or an editorial clearly related to the issue you care about, such as the latest case of egregious tax cuts without offsetting curbs on spending. Begin your letter or e-mail with a quick reference to the relevant article. Send it off immediately with your name, address, and phone number. If it arrives more than 24 hours after the article appeared, it may be deemed too old for publication. Don't expect to hear from the paper unless your letter makes the cut. If it does, don't be surprised to see a shorter version in print.

Here's a sample letter:

To the Editor:
I am dismayed that your newspaper would take such an
irresponsible attitude toward our $7 trillion national debt
(Editorial, June 2). Surely you know that already huge interest
payments on the debt are forcing Congress to make cuts in
vital programs affecting our environment and the education of
our children. If inflation begins to rise even moderately, or if
foreign investors decide to stop lending us money through their
purchases of U.S. Treasury notes and bonds, interest rates will
go up. Higher rates will, in turn, expand the interest payments
we must make on the debt, effectively crippling our government.
Not only are we gambling with our current well-being, we are
risking the future by allowing our government to pursue these
irresponsible fiscal policies.

Many newspapers encourage readers to submit articles for the op-ed page that allow the writer to express detailed opinions in about 700 well-chosen words. Check a paper's Web site for guidelines, or call the editors of its editorial page. Again, timeliness is important. For example, you might submit your op-ed article about the deficit a week or two before Congress is scheduled to release its budget resolution for the next fiscal year. Allow ample time for the newspaper's editors to call you to discuss any questions or problems they have with the piece prior to publication.

Editors expect op-ed authors to have some expertise in the topic they choose to write about. That doesn't mean you have to be an economist or accountant. But you do need a way of catching a busy reader's attention. For example, you can personalize the issue. Your article might describe the ghastly fate of your household budget if you and your family behaved like the drunken sailors currently managing the national budget. If you put the issue in personal terms, your neighbors will listen to you far more attentively than if you pontificate about complex economic concepts.

Radio and television stations carry their own editorial content in the form of segments stating the owners' views on various issues. You can lobby your stations with letters and phone calls, urging them to take a strong position against deficit financing. The stations also conduct interviews with knowledgeable local citizens who hold strong opinions on important local and national matters. Find out if they would be willing to interview you about the debt-and-deficit spiral. If you do get a chance to appear on a radio or television broadcast, bone up on your facts well beforehand and be ready to answer tough, probing questions from your interviewer.

If stations in your area broadcast weekly programs on public affairs, ask the people in charge to schedule a talk show on the spiraling dangers posed by the national debt. Make a similar pitch to local newspapers, suggesting an investigative series on how the national-debt crisis is already boosting local property taxes and weakening your town economy. You can also do local media and yourself a favor by compiling a fact sheet that editors and reporters can use in handling fiscal stories.

- *Speak out.* Given your growing knowledge about the national debt and your escalating concern about its consequences, you can become a spokesperson for balanced budgets and debt reduction. Opportunities abound, particularly among organizations that meet regularly and need speakers with a fresh topic and convincing style. All sorts of groups—civic, professional, religious—might be receptive to your offer to speak, especially if you're perceived as a person who knows much but speaks crisply and is funny as well as scary.

Start with groups you know because you belong to them—your college alumni club, for example. Next, ask your local library, newspaper, or Chamber of Commerce for leads on who's in charge of programming at other organizations. Send them proposals spelling out your topic and its relevance to their particular members. Give your talk a compelling title—not "The National Debt" (yawn), please, but something more apt to make throats dry and palms wet. "Your Government Is Stealing You Blind" may be a bit over the top, at least for a debut talk, but "The National Debt As Terrorism" isn't entirely far-fetched. Don't forget to include a description of yourself, your role in the community, and your in-depth knowledge of the topic.

When a program person shows interest, ask about the group's members. What's their dominant characteristic—conservative, liberal, young, old, apathetic, involved, blue-collar, white-collar? The more you sense people's dreams, fears, and values, the better you can tailor your argument to their interests and concerns. A roomful of Rotarians, for example, is likely to see America differently from a roomful of aging Vietnam War protesters. On the other hand, the national-debt crisis touches all Americans to the point that a rousing talk about it should easily cross all barriers, whether political, racial, economic, religious, or generational. If this isn't Topic A in your town, it won't take much to make it so. Just recite the facts and watch the blood rise in every face in the audience.

Leave time for a question-and-answer session. That's your chance for feedback on your performance. Questions reveal skeptics, converts, fence-sitters. Your answers can allay doubts, win supporters, and show you how to sharpen your next appearance. Your goal is to send your listeners away fuming over the government's fiscal idiocies and not only eager to do something, but convinced that even one person can make a difference. Have a sign-up sheet available for those interested in joining the anti-debt struggle.

- *Petition.* Embedded in the Constitution is the right of Americans to "petition the government for a redress of grievances" (First Amendment). As old as the republic is, petitioning is still an effective method for letting presidents and legislators know they're out of step with thousands of constituents. It also enables even one person to rouse many others with a reasonable investment of time and energy.

The message atop your petition to your elected representatives should be short, to the point, and easily understood. It might read something like this:

> The $7 trillion national debt represents a terrible threat to
> the future of our country. As concerned citizens, we want the
> President and Congress to stop their reckless behavior and act
> now to halt deficit spending and start reducing the national
> debt. We urge you and all the nation's political leaders to put
> America back on a path of fiscal responsibility.

Under the message, leave room for people to write their names and addresses in a lined format. Then make copies, attach them to clipboards, and enlist friends and family to gather names. Discuss with them the language they should use in approaching people. Most people you and your group will talk to probably won't be familiar with the risk posed by the soaring national debt, so you will need to devise a simple, convincing introductory explanation.

You can seek signatures in parks and other public places, or by going door-to-door in neighborhoods. Before you begin canvassing your neighbors, check to see if your town requires you to register with the local police department or town hall. Some localities require registration merely as a precaution against burglars who knock on doors just to find out who isn't home. With the permission of the owners, you can also solicit signatures in shopping malls or factories.

Ideally, you should end up with hundreds—maybe even thousands if your group is large and dedicated enough—of signatures and addresses that can then be delivered to the President and your legislators, either by mail or in person.

Organizing a petition drive is just one of the public methods you can adopt to raise a red flag about the debt issue. You can also organize a meeting, a rally, or a parade. Choose the date with care. If you are supporting or opposing an official because of his or her votes on the budget, aim for the final weeks before an election. Otherwise, time the event to fall just before or just after the announcement of the latest congressional budget resolution.

Prepare banners, posters, and informative handouts to be used at the event. Arrange for any permits or security people required by your community. If speakers will be a part of the gathering, make sure they're well-informed on the debt issue and lively in front of an audience. Remember to alert local organizations to the event so they can encourage their members to attend, and keep feeding press releases highlighting the progress of your program to the local newspaper, radio, and television outlets. Call the day before your event and talk to an editor about assigning a reporter to cover it.

In this, as in all such efforts, it is essential for you to end your event with a call to action. Tell your listeners and readers what they can do to jolt government leaders from their current deep sleep.

Having read this far, you presumably share my alarm about the fiscal train wreck that looms only minutes ahead in America's future. Do I believe it can be stopped before a sickening crash that destroys our economy—indeed our country? Yes, I do—that's why I wrote this book. How to stop the crash has become a passion that fires my life and work. But success requires help from you, tens of thousands of you, a sea of devoted citizens armed with a mighty cause, faith in democracy, and the amazing new tools of public persuasion. There is still time—not much, but enough to fight and win. We begin in a crucial election year, one that will change national history for good or ill. Never let it be said that any of us stood idly by, watching others shape that history. You and I will deserve the country we fight for.

EPILOGUE

I place economy among the first and most important virtues, and public debt as the greatest danger to be feared.

—Thomas Jefferson

AT THE BEGINNING of this book, I recounted Alexander Tytler's grim dictum that all democracies die of greedy citizens plundering the public treasury. In America's own democracy, the jury is still out. Greed and self-interest still flourish, especially among our leaders, blinding many to the world beyond their noses. Yet I am convinced that the worst needn't happen—*if* Americans wake up in time to throw off the yoke of apathy and dependence that is leading to our great nation's decline and fall.

What will it take for us to save ourselves? How can we wean our politicians from profligate spending and their addiction to binge borrowing? How can we avoid a financial crash that would trigger national poverty and world chaos?

The war before us could be our last. It is the war to live within our means, to rebalance the budget, to stop killing off our future. No previous war has entailed higher stakes: Defeat this time might well destroy the American Dream, reducing us to the economic status of a third-rate country begging for foreign aid.

Make no mistake about it: The obstacles to victory are enormous. They begin with our own mass complacency. Too many of us assume the mighty dollar is immortal, ordained by God to last forever. That is not so. Each of us must recognize the truth, and share it with others, until we reach a critical mass that will force our leaders to do the right thing.

Somehow, we must dodge the bullet of higher interest rates speeding toward us. If you remember only one of my dictums, make it this: If we never borrowed another nickel, interest rates rising to 18 percent would eat up all of the government's current income tax revenues just to pay interest on today's national debt. Only 20 years ago, interest rates were *higher* than that.

The situation is already worsening. Interest rates are rising. Inflation is again rearing its head. Our federal government spends far in excess of what it takes in and continues to borrow record amounts, forcing the national debt ever higher. Like the blind leading the blind, President Bush and Congress go on voting for additional benefits, entitlements, and giveaways with no notion of how to pay for them, thus guaranteeing still more debt in the years ahead.

Time is short. No one can say when a crisis will be reached, when an economic trigger will be pulled.

But we aren't helpless. Americans must insist that our leaders be strong, courageous, and resolute. They must cut spending. They must resist the siren call of pork-barrel legislation and giveaways from the public coffers. They must reduce, and eliminate, the annual budget deficit. They must make the hard choices that will salvage Social Security and Medicare, even if it means reducing benefits and restricting beneficiaries.

I have, in this book, provided the facts, the strategy, the tools of our economic salvation. Now we must put them to use.

Page numbers of charts appear in italics.